RÉGION OU TERRITOIRE : F.F.A.

PLACE DE : Fritzlar

CORPS OU SERVICE : 5e Hussards

GUERRE - AIR - MARINE (¹) CARNET SERIE No 6

SOUS-OFFICIER - HOMME DE TROUPE MARIN (¹)

PERMISSION - PROLONGATION DE PERMISSION

devra passer à ... au retour le 19/4/...

ACCORDÉ(E) A :

NOM, PRÉNOMS : TARDI René

GRADE OU EMPLOI : Adjudant Chef

DURÉE (2) : 23 Jours (vingt trois)

VALABLE DU (3) : 28-3-52 AU 19-4-52 INCLUS

POUR ALLER DE (4) : Fritzlar A (5) Valence (Drôme)

96 Rue du Chateauvert

AVEC SOLDE DE (4) : Présence

(7) : _____

A SP 52005 LE 26 Mars 1952

LE (8) Colonel Bernard Colt 5e Hussards

Signature :

29.3.52

FEUILLE...

VISA DU MEDECIN
constant que le titulaire n'est atteint d'aucune maladie contagieuse.

2e ET 3e CLASSES SEULEMENT
SAUF AUTORISATION SPÉCIALE

(1) Rayer les mots inutiles.
(2) Indiquer en toutes lettres le nombre de jours.
(3) Date.
(4) Localité de départ.
(5) Localité de destination, en précisant l'adresse et le département. Si l'intéressé désire bénéficier de sa permission ou de son congé dans plusieurs localités, celles-ci doivent être inscrites par les soins de l'autorité militaire au moment de l'établissement du présent titre ; cette prescription ne concerne pas les aspirants, adjudants-chefs et adjudants ni les sous-officiers de carrière, rengagés ou engagés rentrant d'un territoire de l'Union française ou d'un T.O.E
(6) De présence ou d'absence.
(7) Indiquer, le cas échéant, à l'encre rouge « Est autorisé à revêtir la tenue civile ».
(8) Désignation de l'autorité.

Le présent titre est seul utilisé aussi bien pour les permissions de longue durée que pour celles de courte durée (24 ou 48 heures). Aucun autre modèle de permission ne confère le droit au tarif militaire sur les chemins de fer (en particulier le modèle de petit format utilisé pour les permissions de très courte durée à l'intérieur de la localité où se trouve l'unité dont relève le bénéficiaire).

5e REGIMENT DE HUSSARDS

CERCLE MESS
DES
S/OFFICIERS

* * *
*

1e MAI

INAUGURATION

ONGLET MOBILE - (I)

NOTA :
Le présent onglet doit être rempli par les soins de la mairie (commune ne comptant pas de garnison ni de brigade de gendarmerie) et expédié immédiate-

NOM ET PRÉNOMS : _____
GRADE OU EMPLOI : _____
CORPS OU SERVICE : _____

A (2) _____ est en PERMISSION - en prolongation de PERMISSION - en CONGÉ (I)

RÉGION OU TERRITOIRE : _____

_____ le _____ 19_____

Signé : (4)

(1) Rayer la mention inutile

HAUT COMMISSARIAT DE LA RÉPUBLIQUE FRANÇAISE EN ALLEMAGNE

MODELE 1

COMMANDEMENT EN CHEF FRANÇAIS EN ALLEMAGNE

BAD-KREUZNACH, le 6 mars 1951 -

DEUXIEME CATEGORIE

AUTORISATION DE RÉSIDENCE

N° 87398

(1) { EN ZONE FRANÇAISE D'OCCUPATION
DANS LE SECTEUR FRANÇAIS DE BERLIN

Monsieur TARDI René
(Nom et prénoms)

GRADE ou QUALITÉ : Adjudant - Chef

SERVICE ou AFFECTATION : 3ème R.S.A.

est autorisé à faire venir sa famille composée de :

Nom et prénoms	Date et lieu de naissance	Degré de parenté	Observation
TARDI Henriette née : COLLIN	3. 4.1916 MARSAZ (Drôme)	épouse	Ne pas omettre de mentionner les enfants accompagnant les pa...
TARDI Jacques	30. 8.1946 VALENCE (Drôme)	fils	

VALIDITÉ PERMANENTE A COMPTER DU sept mars 1951 - (en toutes lettres)

LE HAUT COMMISSAIRE DE LA REPU...
FRA...

Le Général d'Armée KOEN...
Commandant en Chef Français en Alle...
Par délégation :

ZONE D'OCCUPA... Le Général de Division CHER...
Commandant Militaire de la Nord

Cherrières

Pièce à conserver par l'intéressé
Voir avis au dos

Nom et Prénoms. : TARDI René

Grade : Adjudant-Chef - Arme Blindée et Cavalerie - Activ...

Affectation actuelle : 8è Région - S.E.P.R. - B.S. No 581 - VALENCE.

Affectation nouvelle : F.F.ALLEMAGNE - 3è Régiment de Spahis Algériens - (Encadrement du 5è Régiment de Hussards)

5e REGIMENT DE HUSSARDS.

N° 142 / 5e Hus /S.A.

NOTE DE SERVICE

L'Adjudant-Chef TARDI, et...

l'échelon Régimentaire , seront mis...

Ier Septembre 51 à 6 heures, 42 de F...

DESTINATION : 53e Bataillon Médical à B...

MISSION : Prendre livraison de trois a...

mécanique, afin d'embarquement le 3 Se...

Les numéros matricules seront remis a...

chargé de l'embarquement de ces derni...

sence pour effectuer 30 Kms.

S.P. 52 7...

DESTINATAIRES/
Adjt-Chef Tardi pour éxecution
Brig- BOULAND " "
Brig-Chef GOULET " "
Archives.

I, RENÉ TARDI, PRISONER OF WAR IN STALAG IIB

TARDI

TRANSLATION BY JENNA ALLEN

COLORS BY JEAN-LUC RUAULT

VOLUME THREE

AFTER THE WAR

FANTAGRAPHICS BOOKS

I'd fought, goddammit! Defeated, but I'd fought! I'm not ashamed. At 3:00 a.m. on May 19th — three days before I was taken prisoner — the general of the 2nd Armored Division hopped in a civilian car on the road out of Cambrai and fled. Then he vanished into the crowd of refugees. That was my general!!! I stayed on the field where, on the banks of the Sambre-Oise Canal, a Kraut cannon was waiting for my partner and me.

Isn't the French Army wonderful!

Driving forward at top speed, we crushed the men manning the small anti-tank gun on the bank of the canal. Then we stopped, our legs turned to jelly.

From my seat at the turret, I saw blood smeared on our treads and the pulpy mass of Germans behind us. Disemboweled, their pearly guts glistened faintly in the May sun. I wanted to vomit!

My partner restarted the tank by himself. We never spoke to each other about what we did there. We were captured the next day.

I never thought about that day while I was at the *Stalag*, but after I returned home, I relived that nightmare every night.

The day I returned home, May 23rd, Himmler had the only good idea of his career: to swallow a cyanide pill. Too bad he didn't think of it earlier!

During our long trek home from Pomerania, I once had the chance to sleep with a buddy in an abandoned house, in a real bed. Two of us under a damp eiderdown that weighed a ton!

I felt oppressed. I was too hot and I felt like I was falling down a well. That goddamn eiderdown weighed down my chest. I couldn't breathe, I was going to drown — and I was sinking into the too-soft mattress.

That night, I had to sleep on the ground. After five years of snoozing on boards, it had become difficult for me to sleep in a bed, under covers so heavy... But that didn't last long. I quickly got back into the habit of a bed, for reasons you can imagine.

Papa, go to sleep or get into bed!

Saint-Marcel-lès-Valence. The city hall had shut down two years earlier, while I was freezing in the *Stalag*. It's May '45 and I'm back in the boondocks after an endless captivity that I could've happily gone without!

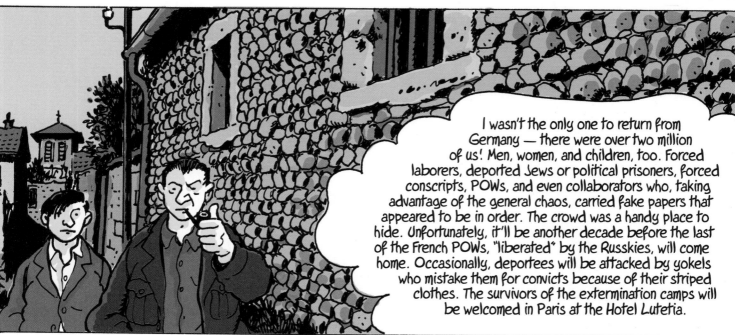

I wasn't the only one to return from Germany — there were over two million of us! Men, women, and children, too. Forced laborers, deported Jews or political prisoners, forced conscripts, POWs, and even collaborators who, taking advantage of the general chaos, carried fake papers that appeared to be in order. The crowd was a handy place to hide. Unfortunately, it'll be another decade before the last of the French POWs, "liberated" by the Russkies, will come home. Occasionally, deportees will be attacked by yokels who mistake them for convicts because of their striped clothes. The survivors of the extermination camps will be welcomed in Paris at the Hotel Lutetia.

There will be all sorts of acts of revenge, not a pretty sight. For sleeping with the enemy, women were shaved, an iron cross was painted on their heads, and they were exhibited for public humiliation. Denunciations were made, sometimes just to get rid of a pesky business rival! Summary executions of collaborators, acts of revenge, half-assed plans, all those sorts of things brought about by the situation.

France had "won" the war! It was all about the FFI*, the 2nd Armored Division, and de Gaulle. The rest of us, who that bastard Marshal had called his "beloved children," we were held responsible for the defeat and the Occupation — that was all our fault!

Even the black market, which had allowed the BECs** and the petty crooks to make a mint, that was our fault too... Anyway. I reunited with Zette, who had waited for me. It must be said that after five years of separation, many couples fell flat on their face and there were a number of divorces. I also reunited with my parents. The Post Office was in the middle of town.

*The French Forces of the Interior, a coalition of French Resistance forces led by General Charles de Gaulle.
**Frenchmen who struck it rich selling butter, eggs, and cheese on the black market. See Volume 1, p. 34.

The last one in the bottom row is my old man.

I already told you that my father, Paul, was born in Corsica, in Venzolasca, a small town south of Bastia. He came to the mainland before the First World War. He got married and had a kid in 1915 — me! He returned from the front disgusted by war. He had been wounded several times, then gassed. He wasn't happy at all with what they had subjected him to!

He was a cobbler and then a postman at the foot of Mount Ventoux, then at Rousset-les-Vignes, in the Drôme region (where I was born), and then here, at St. Marcel. All those routes, all those country roads, in the rain or scorching heat — on a bicycle, too!

My mother came from Valréas, in the Vaucluse region. She was a postlady — stern and thrifty.

So my parents were civil servants — down to their bones! For them, there was nothing better than an orderly life. You know exactly how much you'll make each month. You can predict the future. You can put your savings into an account at the mutual bank — that'll make you a little money. And they were first in line to know about that. Plus, they knew the exact total for retirement, which would come in due course... It was reassuring. They were not adventurous. They didn't understand there were other ways to live.

After returning from war, my father withdrew into himself while remaining very authoritarian. We didn't get along very well, as I mentioned before.

As an only child, I was on the front line. My mother never said a word. Our family home was restrictive, oppressive, mediocre, and perpetually tense. All of that had something to do with my longing to pack up and join the army in '35!

Papa, don't you think that the atmosphere of a barracks is the worst thing in the world?

Doesn't that remind you of something?

?

*The song René sings here is "Ça Sent Si Bon La France" ("France Smells So Lovely"), popularized by Maurice Chevalier in 1941.

In '36 it was still possible to thrash them good, but on March 7th, when a single Boche division penetrated into the Rhineland, we stupidly didn't move an inch, even though we had more than a dozen divisions at the border!

But why did Hitler want to get into the Rhineland so badly?

It was a DMZ, a strip of land 50 km wide, on the right bank of the Rhine and on the left bank to the Franco-Belgian border. The DMZ was established following the Locarno Treaties, signed in 1925, and was meant to protect us and Belgium from possible invasions — the Boche were fond of those! Hitler's success wasn't guaranteed. We might have been able to push him back and end Nazi Germany right then and there, but, of course, we let our chance pass by! What's more, we couldn't do a thing without agreement from our Brit allies, who were on vacation playing golf... What a shitty weekend!

There you go, all worked up!

With good reason! ... I have a toothache, too.

In 1935, Hitler re-established compulsory military service — which had been forbidden by the Treaty of Versailles — and swelled his army to 500,000 men and equipped them with tanks, planes, and cannons. All that with no regard for the peace treaty... We just let him do it!

We had signed a mutual assistance pact with the Soviets, in case the Krauts attacked the east. Hitler contended that the agreement presented a danger to the Reich, giving him the pretext for his show of force, in violation of the Locarno Treaties that Germany had signed!

To wash away the humiliation of the Treaty of Versailles and to reoccupy annexed territories, the living space the Boche needed: these were Hitler's obsessions. These aims, along with many other projects he had under his hat, drove him to invade the Rhineland. We didn't budge when there was a single *feldgrau* in front of us, and we wouldn't move again once the Boche took the region.

The Treaty of Versailles had all the ingredients necessary for a new war!

Our allies, the Czechs, Poles, Russians, Romanians, and Yugoslavs soon realized that now that the Rhineland was fortified and militarized, we would no longer be able to enter the area easily. We hadn't entered when it was possible... How idiotic! Millions of deaths followed! But we felt safe — after all, before us was the "uncrossable" Maginot Line!

I've had it with the Rhineland!

Well, here's the end of the village. Nothing more to see. Let's cross here. That's Jeanne and Dédé Robichon's house. Cousins. Dédé was a tank man, too. He was demobilized at the armistice.

On the training field in '35, we felt all-powerful and invincible during our shooting drills — amidst the sound of our antiquated tanks' engines groaning, the smell of fuel, hot oil, exhaust, and the din of the cannons in action. Goes without saying that five years later, I was quick to see my error in judgment.

In '37, Zette and I married. We moved to Valence, next to the barracks. Two years before the debacle!

St.-Marcel-lès-Valence (population, 937), a small town in the Drôme region without much charm, spread along the two sides of the road from Valence to Romans-sur-Isère. We were in the foothills of the Alps, among fruit trees, in the Rhône Valley, where the mistral winds blow fiercely and drive you mad. St.-Marcel-lès-Valence didn't have much of a town center: just a village square, a few cafés, a boules court, and a fountain — not much fun! Mrs. Archibald's* grocery store is right at the entrance of town when you're coming from Valence.

Seems like a real tourist brochure.

You remember that tall, skinny guy we met at the camp in Triers, at *Dulag* XIID, where we passed through before being sent to Pomerania?
... He was a doctor. In Lyon, I think.

*Berthe Archibald, Zette's mother, is introduced in Volume 1, p. 22.

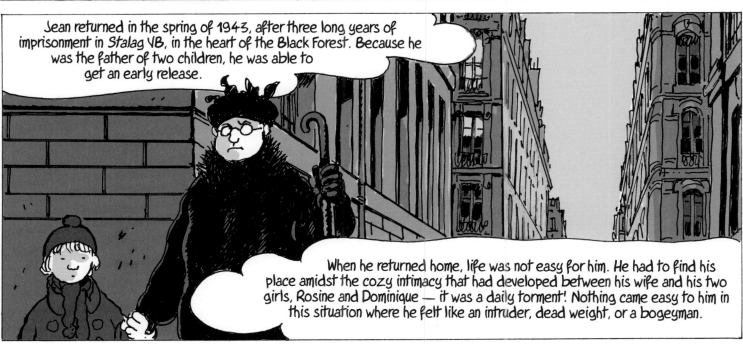

15

HERE HE COMES, THE GREAT WAR HERO, TO SIT AT OUR TABLE!

At the moment, the family is still living for a time with Jean's parents, in Vassieux, near Lyon.

Meals with the grandfather are often tense. He considers the French POWs nothing more than losers. Not like him, a veteran of the Great War, who had been at the Battle of the Aisne! The girls don't understand what he's talking about, but they feel the tension when Monique looks sadly at Jean's gaunt face, his features hollowed by hunger and suffering...

CHEERS TO THE LOSERS!

One day, Monique is frightened badly. Rosine drank the tadpole water, and now she's going to get typhoid! Monique is beside herself. Wild with worry, Jean curtly intervenes, slaps his daughter, then puts her in the corner of the library, alone, and forbids her to leave.

16

Rosine cries and hears her sister crying, too, behind the door... So young, Dominique doesn't understand the violence, dormant until now, but suddenly she hears in her mind an echo of her grandmother's warning: "When he gets back, he'll punish you!"

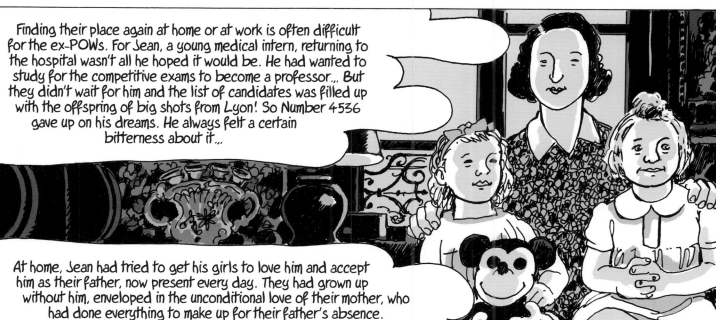

Finding their place again at home or at work is often difficult for the ex-POWs. For Jean, a young medical intern, returning to the hospital wasn't all he hoped it would be. He had wanted to study for the competitive exams to become a professor... But they didn't wait for him and the list of candidates was filled up with the offspring of big shots from Lyon! So Number 4536 gave up on his dreams. He always felt a certain bitterness about it...

At home, Jean had tried to get his girls to love him and accept him as their father, now present every day. They had grown up without him, enveloped in the unconditional love of their mother, who had done everything to make up for their father's absence.

For years Dominique will vividly recall the long, bony hands of this stranger who sometimes held her and Rosine against his chest for a long time, as if trying to recapture what the years of war and captivity had stolen from him: their first smiles, their first steps, their first words...

The post-war years were hard. There were still restrictions, food rations, gas generators. Mrs. Archibald was a tyrant in her grocery store. She was a good woman, but stern, without an ounce of humor or imagination.

That's a Roitelet, the first version.

Berthe Archibald was the widow of Célestin, the barber, father of Zette's half-brother, Basile. She had a brother, Fernand, who was brimming with cleverness, engineering genius, and know-how. He fell into motorcycles and airplanes.

Berthe's second brother, Albert, never came back from the trenches. As for Fernand, he was at Verdun, like everyone else. At the bottom of a shell hole, he had inhaled a big breath of mustard gas. He was evacuated from the front. Fernand asked to be transferred to aviation, where he became an instructor, given his mechanical ability. He rubbed shoulders with Nungesser and Fonck, the ace pilots.

Demobilized in 1918, he went back to Romans, to his repair shop for motorcycles, motors, and automobiles. He upgraded everything upgradable: At the age of 14, he had already built a steam engine — which soon explodes — to turn the millstone on his parents' oil mill. Following the explosion, he installs a gas engine in the mill and, later, an electric engine — this is 1907.

Fernand Bert — Bert was his last name — now devotes himself to the construction of delivery tricycles, for which he had developed a few prototypes in 1910, at 17! He is an ingenious handyman, an inventor, a pioneer, a nonpareil mechanic!

← Fernand

Albert

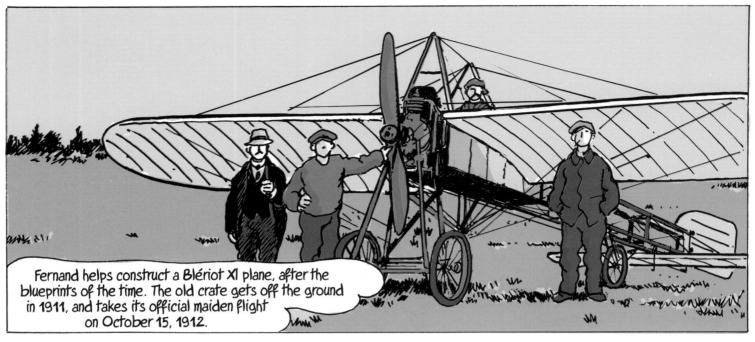

Fernand helps construct a Blériot XI plane, after the blueprints of the time. The old crate gets off the ground in 1911, and takes its official maiden flight on October 15, 1912.

In 1928, he motorizes the delivery tricycles, which are named after him: Bert Tri-Cars, patented in 1929. They're popular among business-owners: grocers, bakers, dairymen, who deliver to homes or places out in the sticks.

He gives up his repair shop and dedicates himself to the mass production of the Tri-Cars. Aeronautics continues to inspire him. Meanwhile, he has two sons: Roger in 1917 and André in 1920. He refuses to license his patent to a motorcycle company, and financial problems soon follow.

Fernand enters the local aviation scene with the creation of a Flying Club on the new airfield. He volunteers to work on engines for aircrafts like the Caudron Luciole, the Potez 36 and the 60, the Farman, the Morane 230, the Caudron Phalène, and the Salmson Cri-Cri.

Here he is in 1936, head mechanic and instructor for the local chapter of the Flying Club in Romans, which aimed to train student pilots for the French Air Force.

May 12, 1940.

Hiding under the belly of the tank, we were relatively protected. But where were Guynemer's* magnificent heirs? Not a single French fighter in the sky! Did the legendary heroism of their glorious predecessor weigh so heavily on their wings that they couldn't take flight? There were a few deaths, including the battalion commander's, and two or three injured. But there weren't any civvies in the area.

As for the anti-aircraft troops, their motto was "Uselessness above all"!

Fernand competes in races to promote his Tri-Cars. Despite breaking records, he soon stops manufacturing the Tri-Cars.

He'll then undertake the construction of the Roitelet, an aircraft of his own invention.

*Georges Guynemer, the ace French fighter pilot. See the glossary entry for p.40 in Volume 1.

Then Roger took his turn: In '36, he builds a type of "Flying Flea," earns his mechanic certificate in '37, then his pilot license in '38.

War... again! Father and sons are mobilized, then demobilized in '40. Roger goes back to the shop and works with his old man. The region was in the non-occupied zone, but in '43 the Boche occupy the rest of France from north to south and establish obligatory work duty. To avoid being sent to slave away in Germany, Roger is forced to abandon the shop. In '44, he joins the Resistance.

In the Resistance, his skills as a mechanic are also greatly appreciated. The Fritz will rob his shop.

During the war, my weapon will be a wrench instead of a rifle!

Upon my return, I reported to my unit — don't forget I'm still a soldier. I had earned 15 days of leave — that was worth the effort of five years in the *Stalag*! The army doctor — who sponged off *Berthe* — extended my leave to 30 days. That was REALLY worth the pain of five years in the *Stalag*! What with the digestive issues, the weight loss, the weakness...

Soon, I was nursing my health at Mrs. Archibald's store, where Zette had spent the entire war. At least she didn't starve. When you live in the country, there's always a chicken egg to eat or a cheese rind to gnaw on.

You already told me that!

Damn! My teeth hurt!

Basile cut hair in his father's little barbershop, built in the courtyard next to the washhouse, behind the grocery. There were no toilets in the house, but in the back of the garden, near the trash cans, a wooden outhouse fulfilled that function. In the winter, you froze your ass off.

Basile told me he had gone to compulsory work duty out of "fear of possible retaliation against his family." So he found himself a hairdresser in Germany, in the shop that belonged to a barber who had permanently given up his clippers, his razor, and his trade — at the bottom of a shell hole. Basile lived with the barber's widow, above the shop, and shared a room with the children. The eldest boy, a nice kid (apparently), always returned from his Hitler Youth indoctrination sessions acting utterly fanatical, elated, and stupefied.

CLACK CLACK CLACK

At the end of the garden, the valleys — and beyond, the Alps.

God, I hate the country!

Me too!

Let's beat it. Nothing to do here.

Basile had come back on leave, but he never stepped foot on the land of the "Great Reich" again. He hid.

Near the end of the war, a woman came to see Mrs. Archibald. She was working at the *Kommandantur* in Valence and said she could take care of Basile's work duty papers. (Basile had vanished.) The woman hoped that they would remember her offer, in case she was harassed by the overzealous racial purists. In truth, Berthe didn't know her at all... No one had asked her for anything. When Valence was liberated, she was seen, apparently, sporting a Resistance armband on her left arm!

For many, it was time to get ready for the post-war period. Time to clean up! Watch out for the scissors! Many women will be shaved in public ('til 1948!) by good ol' French folk, enamored by their own heroism. For guys who'd just been sitting on their asses (and those who had made money on the black market), their crusade against "horizontal collaboration" allowed them to get on the right side of history and appear like magnificent Resistance fighters who hadn't squealed in Gestapo basements! Plus, they had to restore their virility, emasculated by the humiliating defeat. So they took it out on the women... Much safer than attacking the *Kommandantur*!

In France, 20,000 women were shaved.

NAZI LOVER

Later, in a Parisian suburb in the '80s, I'll meet a guy who had been a true Resistance fighter. The French police had arrested him, and the Germans had deported him, just two weeks before the Liberation of Paris. The guy had come back, and every morning since then, he watched the rat who had denounced him walk down his street. Right beneath his windows, the rat passed by with a baguette under his arm, on his way back from the corner bakery! But the guy never said a word!

Rotten luck! Ten days before the Liberation of Paris, the police in the capital, after working for the Nazis, heroically joined the Resistance! Yeah, I know there were Resistance cops from the beginning — but still!

In Paris and its suburbs, Operation Spring Breeze came in the early morning on Thursday, July 16, 1942. At the behest of the Germans, in an infamous, boot-licking spirit of collaboration, the secretary general of the Vichy police, René Bousquet, and his minions implemented — enthusiastically! — the arrest of 28,000 Jews, foreigners or of foreign descent, in their homes!

To get the job done, 9,000 French policemen invaded apartment buildings and pounded on the doors of Jews on file. No German soldier needed to participate in the operation... which was reassuring.

May 29, 1942. The German military commander in occupied France has required all Jews, age six and up, to wear the yellow star. Starting June 7th, the star must be worn visibly, sewn tightly on the left side of the chest. You'll be able to pick up a star at the local police station. Every Jew will receive three stars in exchange for one clothes ration stamp.

Some Jews were able to get out in time, because there were leaks — leaflets from the Jewish Resistance and some warnings from the police themselves. But those were rare. In a few cases, neighbors would hide them to keep them safe. Children would be saved, evacuated outside of Paris. But other neighbors applauded, from their windows, the arrest of 3,118 men, 5,919 women, and 4,115 children. "Take the children too!" said Laval.

26

Grouped in different places, these people will board public busses with their bags and suitcases, and then be confined at Drancy, awaiting departure to Auschwitz. (Pets needed to be left with the concierge.) Others, victims of the Vélodrome Roundup*, will travel to the camps at Pithiviers or at Beaune-la-Rolande, then sent to their deaths at Auschwitz.

The orders were carried out by hooded police agents, the Mobile Republican Guard (which maintained public order) and French gendarmes. Cops in uniform and in plain clothes. Some of whom committed the crime with zeal, others with indifference, and still others well aware of what they were doing. A few had tried to warn people but, on the whole, no one disobeyed!

The convoys heading to Pitchipoi followed. "Pitchipoi" was the name that children interned at Drancy had given to that frightening, unknown destination to which they were to be sent without knowing the reason... Pitchipoi!

*See the glossary entry about the Vélodrome Roundup in Volume 2.

I wonder what state of mind those pig bastards were in when they went home to their families, that Thursday evening in July? Were they able to kiss their wives? Plant a gentle kiss on the innocent foreheads of their sleeping children?

13,152 people arrested! Not enough for Bousquet! New roundups were planned. There have been many and there will be more. The Vélodrome d'Hiver, then Drancy, where men, women, and the elderly are crammed into horrific conditions... where, of course, the gendarme ransack packages, steal money, jewelry — anything of value — and fatten their wallets on the black market.

Germany surrenders on May 8th, but the war isn't over. The Americans continue to fight in the Pacific. The Japanese are tenacious.

And the rev, er, pistol from Lüneburg* — what did you do with it?

I hid it!

I really need to see a dentist!

It was already getting unpleasant to live under the same roof as Zette's stepmother — and in a grocery store, no less. We were seriously considering living elsewhere. My leave was ending shortly, and I'd have to rejoin the 504th in Valence. I had no diploma... The damn pencil-pushers had been able to keep studying, so the civil service jobs to help rebuild the nation were already taken. And I, who had signed up in '35 to kick Hitler's ass, I was here, like a moron! Should I stay in the army?

*René salvages this pistol during his return home from the *Stalag.* See Volume 2, p. 108.

In August 1944, Roger had participated in the Liberation of Romans and, later, Lyon. In Romans, there was an American officer, totally lost, caught under German fire with his driver and Jeep. Roger got him back on track. As thanks, the Yank gave him a gift: a wicked little Czech pistol, confiscated from a Kraut officer.

On their way out, the Germans intensified their retaliation against the civilians to prevent us from being too happy about their departure. Massacres at Vassieux-en-Vercors, La Chapelle-en-Vercors, and many other places. They also executed Resistance fighters locked up in Lyon, Grenoble, and Chambéry...

Even here, at St. Marcel, seven imprisoned members of the Resistance were executed on August 23th. The next day, the first American tanks arrived. The Resistance fought alongside them and the town — as well as Valence — was liberated on the 31st.

On April 6, 1944, the Gestapo in Lyon, commanded by *Obersturmführer SS* Klaus Barbie, had rounded up 44 children and their seven teachers from the Jewish orphanage in Izieu, in the Ain region. They had then been sent to Auschwitz, from which they would never return. In '43, Barbie had captured and personally tortured Jean Moulin, the leader of the Resistance, captured in Caluire, a suburb of Lyon!

ABANDONED citizens,

GET OUT!

trust the GERMAN SOLDIERS!

trust the GERMAN SOLDIERS!

trust the GERMAN SOLDIERS!

On June 9th, the first regiment *"Der Führer"*, attached to the *"Das Reich"* division, arrives at Tulle, in the Corrèze region. The commander, *Sturmbannführer SS* Kowalsch, orders the hanging of 99 hostages, payback for the execution of nine German soldiers, shot the night before by the FTP*. They throw the bodies into the river. Militia members in Limoges select 149 residents of Tulle to be deported to Dachau.

On June 10th, a company from the *"Der Führer"* regiment, commanded by *Sturmbannführer SS* Diekmann, arrives at Oradour-sur-Glane, not far from Limoges.

It was the same story as Tulle's: revenge! Oradour was supposedly a Resistance hideout — not true! 241 women and 202 children are burned alive in the church, men are machine-gunned in barns — 642 victims in all! Among the executioners were Frenchmen from Alsace and Lorraine (forcibly enlisted), men from Luxembourg, as well as the *"Volksdeutsche"* (Germans born abroad).

*The *Francs-Tireurs et Partisans*, a Resistance organization formed by the French Communist Party in 1942.

The Panzer Division "*Das Reich*" reaches the front and heads for Normandy, where the Allies landed on June 6th. Under orders from *Brigadeführer SS* Lammerding, *Das Reich* sows a path of terror, leaving a river of blood in its wake. Lammerding, condemned to death in absentia by the Bordeaux court, will deny responsibility for the massacres committed by his men. He will not be extradited from Germany, and he will die peacefully in 1971, at Bad Tölz in Bavaria!

The execution of prisoners, torture, decapitations with sharpened shovels, arrests of Jews... The militiamen are also in the field, but not for long... 6,000 of them will flee to Germany. Some, incorporated into the Charlemagne Division*, will end their days in Berlin.

To a person with shit for brains, certain he belongs to the "superior race", it was "normal" to shoot a bullet point-blank into the head of a communist Pole, or a Russian, or a Roma, or a Jew. To him, that's not murder. He's convinced that he's not killing a human, merely a "sub-human". That's what eased the last shred of conscience that may have still existed in the ugly mug of that executioner!

*A unit of French SS forces. See the glossary entry for p.41 in Volume 2.

Contrary to the image of ruthless, cold-blooded *SS* killers, what folks long would have you believe, many of the young *Wehrmacht* boys gave into the temptation of the excitement they got from the killings.

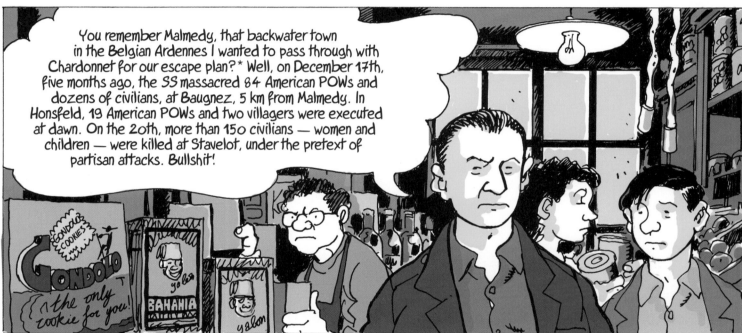

You remember Malmedy, that backwater town in the Belgian Ardennes I wanted to pass through with Chardonnet for our escape plan?* Well, on December 17th, five months ago, the *SS* massacred 84 American POWs and dozens of civilians, at Baugnez, 5 km from Malmedy. In Honsfeld, 19 American POWs and two villagers were executed at dawn. On the 20th, more than 150 civilians — women and children — were killed at Stavelot, under the pretext of partisan attacks. Bullshit!

"From this point forward, the American troops will no longer take *SS* prisoners, and this may well extend to all German soldiers." That wasn't an order, merely a "recommendation" from General Simpson, head of the U.S. Ninth Army.

*René discusses his escape plan with Chardonnet in Volume 1, pp. 147-149.

These massacres, and so many others, delineate the path of the *kampfgruppe* led by *Standartenführer SS* Peiper and his panzers. Peiper cut his teeth in the USSR by razing towns and murdering their people.

The *Das Reich* division was also in the Ardennes but, unlike Lammerding, Peiper will receive a death sentence in 1946. His sentence kindly reduced, he'll only serve 11 years in prison, then he'll discretely move to France, to Traves in the Haute-Saône region. But he knew he was being hunted by former French Resistance fighters — who may have taken care of him on July 14, 1976.

Served him right!

The battle in the Ardennes had been Hitler's last assault. To the east, Ivan was brutally hurtling forward, driven by vicious intent. The second front, from the west — long-awaited by Stalin — marked the end of the Great Reich.

In Moscow, Stalin is pleased. It's the victory parade. On June 24, four years after the German invasion of the USSR and one month after my return, Marshal Zhukov reviews the troops.

Zhukov mounts Kumir, a large, white stallion. Stalin would've loved to be in his place but, during rehearsal, Kumir unseated Stalin and the "Little Father" injured his arm. Was Stalin hoping that Zhukov would bust his head open in the middle of Red Square?

Two hundred flags, banners, standards and other Nazi talismans were burned in front of Lenin's mausoleum at the end of the parade — even the gloves of men who had dabbled in Hitler's atrocities. That was all well and good, but Stalin was himself a monstrous criminal, a merciless enthusiast of torture and deportation.

In other words, a true dictator!

The Nazis weren't the only ones filling communal graves. As early as 1937 (the year I married Zette), at the time of the "Great Terror" and the "Purges," Stalin arbitrarily chose people to send to the gulag camps, those he deemed "individuals detrimental to society," "counter-revolutionaries," "traitors," "saboteurs," or "spies". He also killed an enormous number of people. There were millions of victims! Long after my death, they'll discover these Stalinist mass graves.

I already mentioned Katyn — 22,000 POWs and Polish officers murdered by the NKVD* in 1940. These graves were discovered by Germans throughout the Katyn forest. One bullet in the back of the head, Gestapo-style, to make people believe Nazis had committed the massacre... But it was definitely Stalin's work!

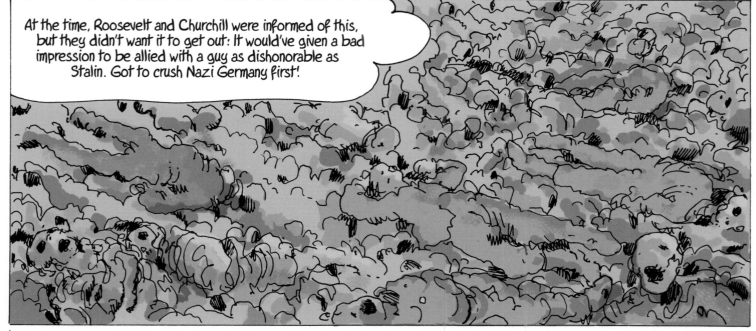

At the time, Roosevelt and Churchill were informed of this, but they didn't want it to get out: It would've given a bad impression to be allied with a guy as dishonorable as Stalin. Got to crush Nazi Germany first!

*The People's Commissariat for Internal Affairs, the Soviet secret police that carried out mass arrests, deportations, and executions until Stalin's death in 1953.

Zhukov entered Berlin on April 27th, proudly riding a T34, fresh out of a Siberian factory. The city fell in early May. Two million German POWs hit the road and headed for captivity.

Given the Krauts hadn't been too kind to the Russkies, the odds were good that the Russkies wouldn't be nice to them. What's more, they seized a million civilians, men and women, to be the workforce for reconstruction — forced labor! The Hiwis, General Vlasov's traitorous army that had joined the Germans, were executed on the spot! Vlasov had finalized an agreement with Himmler in '44 to fight the Bolsheviks. The Americans delivered him to the Russians. He'll be hanged in Moscow.

The Russian POWs, forced to work for the Germans, were "liberated" by the Red Army or the Allies only to be taken straight to the gulag camps for treason, cowardice, disobedience, abandonment of post...

Hitler had imagined a New Berlin, more beautiful than Paris, vast and enduring: Germania! It would be the capital of the world!!! Speer, an architect and his only friend, designed the buildings, mapped out the plans, and constructed a large model according to his master's mad vision. A dome, 300 meters tall, a magnificent central avenue, longer and wider than the Champs-Élysées, an Arc de Triomphe twice as tall as the one in Paris, government offices, oversized Trocadéro plazas all over the place. Zero imagination!

All that mattered: Make it more colossal, more towering, more imposing, more extensive, more overbearing than anything built to date! To build it all, they needed stone and thousands of slaves. The camp prisoners will slave away until their death — like the POWs in Natzweiler-Struthof, in annexed Alsace — to extract Speer's favorite granite from quarries. Greco-Roman rubbish... lousy Parthenons, Pantheons, Vaticans... in pink granite! A backdrop for a dreary German epic. Germania, my ass!

Unter den Linden, Wilhelmstrasse, Alexanderplatz, Friedrichstrasse, Postdamer Platz, the Führer's Chancellery — ruins... ruins... ruins... All of Berlin reduced to 200 square kilometers of rubble! Well, in 1935 hadn't Hitler declared: "In 10 years, Berlin will be unrecognizable"?

Posters read: "Soldier of the Red Army, you are now on German soil: The hour for revenge has come!" The Russkies completely dismantled the German factories and sent the machinery to the USSR. Stalin's field marshals no longer knew how to fulfill orders for Mercedes placed by Moscow. Property was shipped by truck to Russia (as the Germans had done to the countries they'd occupied). The average soldier swiped faucets, toilet flushes, kitchen utensils, and electric lightbulbs. Amid the chaos, the German women were easy prey, unprotected. Two million German women were raped, from 12 to 80 years old.

Four months ago, the Russians liberated Auschwitz. Three weeks ago, they entered Ravensbrück camp, on the shores of a lovely lake, across from the small city of Fürstenberg.

Ravensbrück was a women's camp. There were about 130,000 women of diverse nationalities, including children — political prisoners, Resistance fighters, outcasts, prostitutes and, of course, Jews and Romani. In the infirmary, monstrous experiments, pointless and purely sadistic, are conducted on "the rabbits" and on babies.

"The rabbits"?

That's what they called the prisoners the SS "doctors" hacked up, amputated, and forced abortions on!

My leave had come to an end and I was back at the barracks of the 504th regiment of Alpine combat tanks.

Alpine?!! Does that mean you put skis on the treads of your tanks when it snowed?

Go ahead, be a smart aleck! Only bumpkins are smart alecks! Jesus H. Christ! You'll see morons like that in the barracks! Shit! It's nauseating! Fucking goddamn bullshit... Makes me want to puke! No wonder we got fucked in the ass!

Oh! What a filthy mouth!

RENÉ!

HA! HA! HA! HA!

Your father came back from captivity very quick-tempered, aggressive, horribly vulgar, and always in a bad mood. I hardly recognized him anymore... At that time, there were a lot of marriages, family reunions, parties... We were often invited out, but he'd never want to go. I'd insist, he would come, and it would always go very badly. René would insult everyone. He'd argue for no reason — with my mother, Basile, his father. He even fought with a cousin who worked at the town hall in Valence.

40

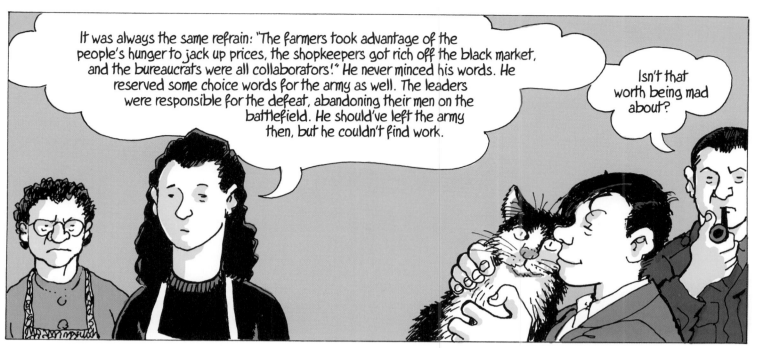

It was always the same refrain: "The farmers took advantage of the people's hunger to jack up prices, the shopkeepers got rich off the black market, and the bureaucrats were all collaborators!* He never minced his words. He reserved some choice words for the army as well. The leaders were responsible for the defeat, abandoning their men on the battlefield. He should've left the army then, but he couldn't find work.

Isn't that worth being mad about?

Second row, fourth from the left: that's me!

What's more, after six years without a drop of alcohol, he became drunk quickly. It all quieted down over time, but that was a difficult period to live through.

Leave the cat alone!

You're forgetting about the alcohol we distilled in the camp with the Americans!* By the way, I wrote to Jack and Kenneth, who had sent me their addresses in the U.S.

*René discusses his distilling career in Volume 1, p. 170.

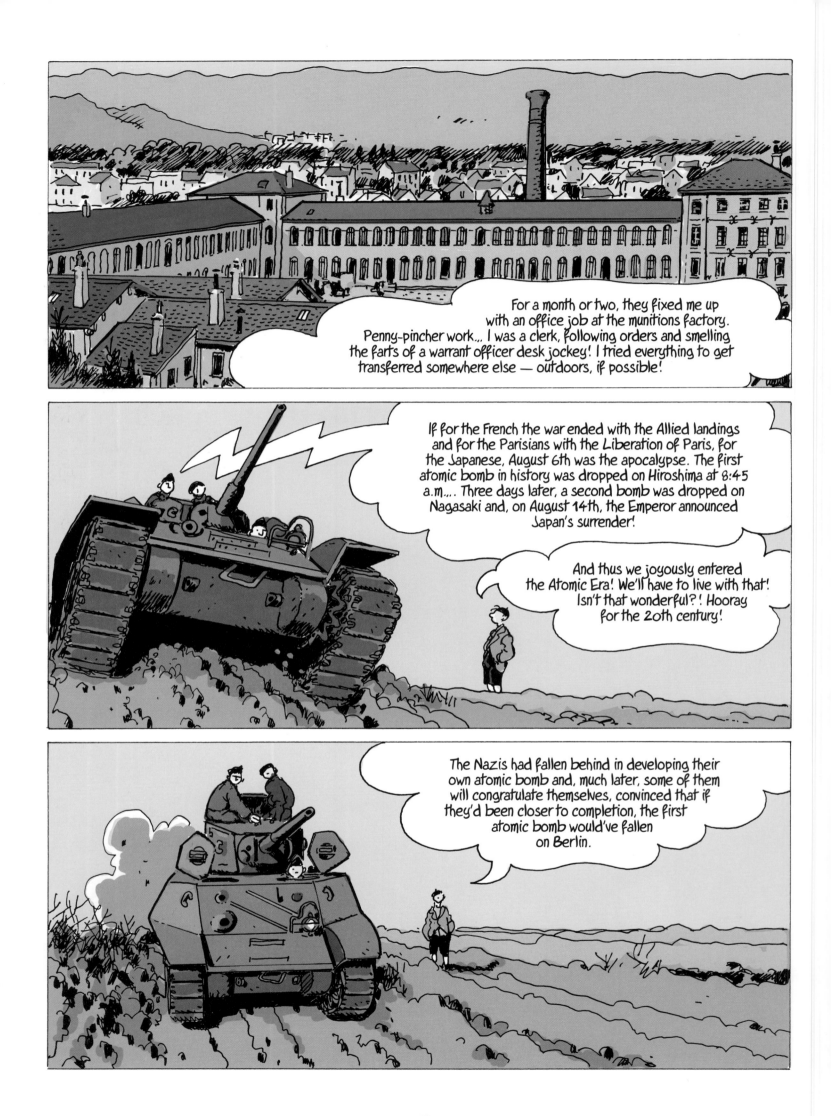

*For more about the involvement of former Nazis in the U.S. space program see the glossary entry for pp. 39-40 in Volume 2.

At the end of summer, "Boy"* — my buddy Drouot — came from Paris with Yvonne and visited us in St. Marcel. They stayed three days at the hotel in Valence. Boy had been back at his job at Hispano-Suiza for a while. Of course we reminisced about the *Stalag*.

On September 7th, a new local paper appeared: *The Free Dauphiné*. At the end of April of the same year, 1945, French women would vote for the first time! One year earlier, in Algiers, a decree from the French Committee of National Liberation, signed by de Gaulle, had granted women the right to vote.

German women got it in 1918, and the English in 1928!

THE free DAUPHINÉ

FRIDAY September 7 1945

THE FREE PAPER FOR FREE MEN

SEPTEMBER 10 — First Peace Conference will be in London

GO WEST, YOUNG MEN, GO WEST!

L'ESPAGNE

Hiroshima devastated by atomic bomb

It's no surprise to me that France, a country convinced it set an example for the whole world, waited so long!

As you know, in 1871, the Paris Commune had already outlawed the death penalty (shortly re-instated by that old maggot, Thiers). It would take a century to reverse that flip-flop!

That wasn't the order of the day! For the time being, we're shooting collaborators. By the way, Pétain received a death sentence on August 15th, but his hide'll be saved by his "heroics" at Verdun and his old age... He'll face life imprisonment!

*René relates the origin of Drouot's nickname in Volume 1, p. 135.

November 20, 1945.
Nuremberg.

Nuremberg — Hitler's "ideological capital,"
as he called it.

The city was bombed as early as 1943. On May 8th and 9th, 335 British bombers arrived and dropped 358 tons of explosives and 412 incendiaries. On August 10th and 11th — 653 bombers, 1,756 tons of bombs (mostly incendiaries). On March 31, 1944 — 795 Lancaster bombers, 2,086 tons of bombs. On April 10th — it kept coming! January 2nd, 1945 — 51 Lancasters, 2,304 tons of bombs. Then, in February, the Americans punched in. On March 16th, the English returned with 301 Lancasters and 40 Mosquitos. The last aerial attack was April 11th, and nine days later, U.S. troops from the Seventh Army occupy Nuremberg! ... Thousands were dead or homeless.

On November 20th, six months after Adolf's suicide, a series of trials for the Nazi criminals began in Nuremberg. The city was in bad shape, but fortunately the Palace of Justice was intact — good news, because the first trial was for the most important Nazi culprits who fell into American hands.

That November, I re-enlisted for a year.

WHAT?!

The trial last from Tuesday, November 20, 1945 to Tuesday, October 1, 1946. After 10 months of debate, 400 hearings, the 22 Nazi criminals were pronounced guilty for instigating the Second World War and for organizing the systematic extermination of the Jews in Europe. They were condemned to "*Tod durch den Strang***", and the sentence was passed 11 times! In German, English, Russian, and even French! Plotting, war crimes, crimes against peace... CRIMES AGAINST HUMANITY. That was the first time, during a trial, that this new legal concept was invoked!

Crimes against humanity! I'm afraid that we'll hear more about that for a long time!

A new word was also coined at Nuremberg: "Genocide," thought up by Raphael Lemkin, a Jewish Polish lawyer.

Genocide? What does that mean?

The word "genocide" was introduced during the bill of indictment.

Génos = tribe or race... Seems like that's Greek? Cide = to kill... That's Latin.

Oh, right! Cide... like homicide, regicide, patricide, insecticide, fratricide, infanticide... Uh...

*German for "Death by hanging."

47

This is how they defined genocide: "The premeditated and systematic extermination of racial and national groups within the civilian population of occupied territories in order to destroy certain races or classes in the population and nation groups, racial or religious, particularly the Jews, Poles, Romani, and others."

Race!! That's a definition we wouldn't use today, since we know that "races" don't exist — but prejudice dies hard!

During the trial, the Americans didn't use the word "genocide," surely because the term made them face the criminal history of their country, built on the backs of black slaves — and the genocide of the Native Americans! Between 80 and 100 million Native Americans starved and murdered (depending on the source)!!

There was a real crowd in the ruins of Nuremberg! Not counting the journalists — 80 Americans, 50 Englishmen, 40 Frenchmen, and 25 Russians. Some of the press covering the event were lodged in Stein, at a castle that belonged to M. Faber-Castell, the pencil maker!

Later, in my own clumsy way, I'll get a lot of use out of these colored pencils!

IMT PRESS CAMP

Here's some buddies and I taking a sidecar motorcycle by storm in the barracks courtyard. I was quite satisfied with my Gnome-Rhône motorcycle. It was a great bike. The Germans thought so, too, and a large number of Gnome-Rhônes were employed in the *Wehrmacht*. They were found all the way to Russia.

The war had come to an end. Roger went back to work at the bicycle and motorcycle repair shop in Romans. He married. He raced "specials" — stock motorcycles modified and improved under his care.

During the war, the airfield was occupied by the *Milice**. They had to get the flying club going again. Roger and his father Fernand continued to build airplanes. Those machines were much thirstier than motorcycles, and fuel was still rare, so there was a move toward gliders.

There will be problems with hoist. Later, a Stampe will be used to tow the gliders. High-altitude flights to treat whooping cough were invented. Roitelet planes built in the Trimotos shop were great fliers.

*A militia created by the Vichy regime in 1943 to combat the Resistance. See the glossary entry for p.41 in Volume 2.

On December 9th, General Patton, accompanied by General Gay and his driver, goes bird hunting in the woods neighboring the city of Speyer. A tanker cuts them off. The impact proves fatal to Patton, breaking his neck, and he dies on the 21st, in Heidelberg.

I still had toothaches! I went to the infirmary. A dentist — more like a mad yanker — systematically pulled all my teeth. The upper and the lower. I remembered the scene when I had my wisdom tooth extracted without anesthesia at the *Stalag* by a Polish doc, and also the Kraut dentist in Bocholt, that fawning ass-kisser who hadn't wanted me to pay with my last "camp marks"** ... I was delighted with my dentures!

Living under the same roof as your mother-in-law is bad for your health! It was time to get out. We rented an apartment on Victor Hugo Road, in the heart of Valence — above a grocery store! Mrs. Archibald helped us financially with the move. She was a good woman.

*René's dental misadventures occur in Volume 1, p. 123 and Volume 2, p. 117, respectively.

The apartment was cramped and uncomfortable, but we made do. It was temporary. And then Zette got pregnant. Baby would come in August.

Aren't you tired of going around in that ridiculous get-up?

So in 1945 there were shaved women, the settling of scores, purging trials around Europe — and colonial massacres in Algeria on May 8th, in Setif, Guelma, Kherrata, and in other places, which were like a few drops of blood compared to a genocide. 45,000 dead! I'll tell you about it later.

In case the German population didn't want to hear about the Nazi concentration camps, movies were made in the camps to take care of that. Hitchcock had overseen the filming of one of those terrifying reports. He had given instructions to the cameramen: long shots with no possibility of cutting, so that no one could say that the film had been tampered with to falsify reality.

But the American and English ministers of foreign affairs had decided not to screen these reports to avoid demoralizing those "good" Germans who needed, instead, to be urged to get the country moving again!

51

Given (1) our shameful behavior during the war, (2) an uncertainty about who we were at the end of it — Resistance fighters? Collaborators? Ethnic cleansers? Communists? — and (3) a lack of confidence in de Gaulle (whose provisionary government wasn't recognized until 1944) — given all that, the Allies had decided in 1942 that France would be occupied and governed by its liberators.

After the German Occupation came the Allied Occupation with a military government, the AMGOT (Allied Military Government of Occupied Territories).

An Occupation currency had already been minted and de Gaulle was displeased, calling our American friends "counterfeiters"! Those lousy bills will stay in the cash registers!

The German POWs were imprisoned in England and in the U.S. until 1944 — and will be repatriated in 1946 — but a million *Wehrmacht* prisoners will stay in France for four years, despite the arguments of the International Committee of the Red Cross. The prisoners were retained for the reconstruction, fieldwork, and — contrary to the Geneva Convention — mine clearing! 34,000 of them will lose their lives. An estimated 30,000 will stay in our beautiful country after 1948.

A bunch of rugrats arrived on the market that year, at the end of that goddamn war that killed 40 million... Was that the exact number? It was like the whole world was putting in overtime to make more cannon fodder for future bloodbaths! Even though Vichy hadn't invented "Mother's Day," a bumper crop of little Pierres popped out in 1946.

Work... Family... Nation.

MOTHER'S DAY
MAY 26 1946
50 Frs
FAMILY BRINGS TOGETHER THE FRENCH PEOPLE

1946's not going well. The bread rations have been reinstated. In Palestine, under British mandate, Zionist groups begin to cause damage in Jerusalem, Tel Aviv, Haifa — 10 victims. Their goal: the creation of a Jewish state in Palestine. The English believe that they had to take Arab interests into account... People start hearing talk about Ho Chi Minh... Churchill, in a speech, talks about an "Iron Curtain" threatening to close off Eastern Europe. New attacks in Palestine!

A French contingent disembarks at Tonkin... 58 prison guards from the Mauthausen concentration camp receive a death sentence... Even more terrorist attacks in Palestine... Walt Disney's feature-length film *Pinocchio* is released in France. In July, a pogrom in Kielce, Poland, kills 41!

The 43 perpetrators of the Malmedy massacre — all SS soldiers, including the *Standartenführer* Joachim Peiper — have just been sentenced to death by the American Military Court in Dachau... Everyone keeps smacking each other around in Palestine, but all that will come to an end soon, I'm sure. The aftermath of the war was rough.

Leave that cat alone!

My father had written to Jack and Kenneth, his moonshine buddies at the *Stalag*. Jack had responded. Maybe he was touched that I was named Jacques, since he sent us several boxes of dry milk for my first bottles.

Watch out for the hypocrites, those magnificent and sincere moralizing types who are always ready to sell their buddies out to the Gestapo! Beware of the born leaders — you'll meet a heap of them. They change sides at just the right moment and then you'll be all alone, like an idiot, on the front line... I wouldn't want to be in your shoes.

Go fuck yourself!

September brings the first Cannes Festival and the first issue of *Tintin* magazine... Shit's hitting the fan in Indochina. The Haiphong Incident: 6,000 dead. Ho Chi Minh leaves Hanoi and calls for revolution. Things aren't going so well in Algeria either... Are these the last days of colonialism?! A bombing in Palestine. A wing of the King David Hotel goes up in smoke: 76 dead. At the United Nations, definitively installed in New York, Belgium files a complaint against Franco for harboring Léon Degrelle, a Nazi. Spain is refused entry into the UN. A resolution to break diplomatic relations with Spain is swiftly adopted.

In October '46, sentenced to death by hanging in Nuremberg, Göring commits suicide in his cell shortly before his execution. At that time, a lot of Nazis were eating cyanide.

What should I talk about? ... Not much is happening right now, except in October my father re-enlisted for two more years!! In January '47, Vincent Auriol became the first president of France's Fourth Republic, and then we moved.

Here we are now in the Châteauvert neighborhood, on Serbia Road, in a rented apartment owned by Mr. and Mrs. Chagrin. I remember that the house was large, with a garden and a veranda, and we lived on the second floor. On the street, next to the front door, there was a mailbox painted blue.

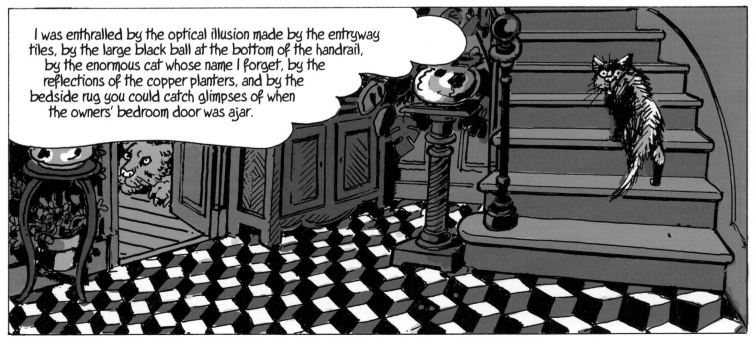

I was enthralled by the optical illusion made by the entryway tiles, by the large black ball at the bottom of the handrail, by the enormous cat whose name I forget, by the reflections of the copper planters, and by the bedside rug you could catch glimpses of when the owners' bedroom door was ajar.

On our floor, there was a communal bathroom with a bidet, a sink, and a bathtub with lion feet. Our squat toilets were on the balcony. So in the winter you had to go outside and freeze your ass off. I slept in my parents' bedroom.

The pelican* had found it's place on a shelf. The furniture was plain and dull. Later, my parents will acquire a "dining room" — sideboard, table, four chairs — in a clunky, over-embellished style, along with a sofa bed covered with brick-red crushed velvet and a radiator with a continuous flame.

The walls of the apartment were bare, but you could admire a chromolithograph of Millet's *The Angelus* pinned up on the bathroom door.

*René explains the origin of the wooden pelican in Volume 1, p. 167. See also the essay in Volume 2, p. 141.

On the balcony, you overlooked the neighborhood. You could see the chimney of the factory next door. I never knew what they made there, in that factory whose siren you heard four times a day during the week. The municipal siren tests on the first Wednesday of the month, at noon, scared my mother stiff... bad memories... It made her think of an alarm, as if Krauts were about to swoop down on my crib!

Every day, when my father came back from the barracks, he'd put on his civvies and go up to the attic. He sat at an old desk turned into a workbench. There, he tinkered with radio sets. One day, he agreed to repair a neighbor's wireless radio and was immediately denounced, accused of moonlighting... "So you can imagine the Occupation!" he said to me much later, when he told me this story.

And then he received a letter from the wife of his old buddy Chardonnet, the fellow prisoner with whom my father had planned to escape. He had been killed in their shack by the Stalag guards, right before their escape.

Chardonnet's wife asked my father if he knew the name of the *posten* that had killed her husband. She had set her mind to finding him and getting him tried for war crimes! Did my father know that guy's name? Did he write back? Alas, I found her letter long after my father's death.

One day my father brought home a white mouse. It lived on the balcony because my mother said it stank. I loved giving it little pieces of gruyere to nibble on. One morning, the mouse had disappeared. The door to the cage my father had made was open... I sobbed. They told me that the owners' fat cat had eaten it. Had the cat opened the door to the cage, too?

Papa spent all day at the barracks. What the heck could he have been doing in a place like that? One day, my mother and I passed by that big building and it left a bad impression on me for a long time. The building scared me. Sometimes, he went on "manoeuvres" for several days. What was that about? He told me that he had been promoted. So now he was a warrant officer... So what? What's a warrant officer?

59

It wasn't until much later, when I stumbled upon some faded and yellowed "Mission Orders," that I got a vague idea of my papa's military doings. It seems that he had been a communications specialist, an instructor, and also a tank commander?! He re-upped for a year in '48 and for another in '49! For the time being, I was drawing on the table in the new dining room, while René was finishing a wooden ship model. He had made each piece according to the plans. My mother had sewn the sails on her sewing machine.

Sometimes, on Sunday, my father didn't go to the barracks. In the afternoon, while my mother did the ironing, he would put on his bicycle clips. Next, we would go down to the garage to get the bicycle and, with me balanced on the bar, we'd ride through the streets, always toward the same destination.

We'd head for the train station. There, we'd go up the metal walkway and watch the trains pass, standing right in the line of the smoke... We'd get a face full of smoke... My father would raise me above the railing so I could get a better look at the big locomotives.

They were high-speed trains, headed down to Marseille or up to Paris. We could see the driver and his mechanic in the cab, just like Jean Gabin and Julien Carrette in that one movie.* They'd be black from coal and scared the crap out of me. I would wave at them anyway... Sometimes they'd wave back. We'd stay a little while longer for the fun of it, and when we'd get bored we'd go home the way we came, with me on the frame.

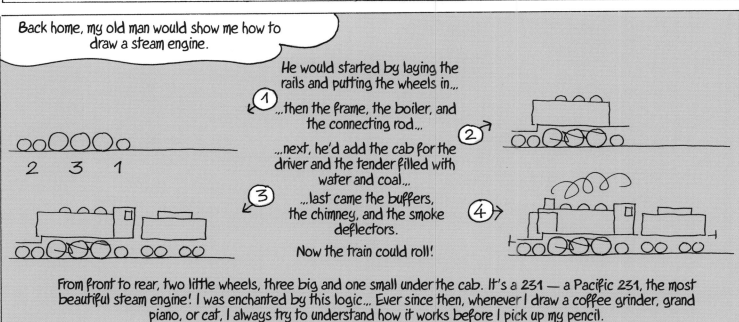

Back home, my old man would show me how to draw a steam engine.

He would started by laying the rails and putting the wheels in...

① ...then the frame, the boiler, and the connecting rod...

② ...next, he'd add the cab for the driver and the tender filled with water and coal...

③ ...last came the buffers, the chimney, and the smoke deflectors.

④

Now the train could roll!

2 3 1

From front to rear, two little wheels, three big and one small under the cab. It's a 231 — a Pacific 231, the most beautiful steam engine! I was enchanted by this logic... Ever since then, whenever I draw a coffee grinder, grand piano, or cat, I always try to understand how it works before I pick up my pencil.

PACIFIC ROSE

Text by Dominique Grange

Art by Tardi

My name is Jerzy Makovski: I was born in Fouquières-lès-lens, in 1898, to Polish immigrant parents.

Much later, I'll illustrate a story, "Pacific Rose," written by Dominique, who, like me, is enamored with steam engines.

*Jacques is referring to the 1938 film *La Bête Humaine*, directed by Jean Renoir.

After completing his three-masted ship, Papa embarked on a tugboat model to make his buddy "Boy" Drouot happy. Drouot's father, in *Le Havre*, was the captain of a similar boat for *Les Abeilles*, a tugboat company. He made the boiler out of a shell case.

My parents, "Boy," and his wife, Yvonne, had gone on a sojourn to the south. I stayed with my paternal grandparents, who now lived in Valence.

In order to go away for a few days, my father had to get his leave papers and take them to the local gendarmerie at his destination.., in case war broke out again — you never know! But why didn't he leave the army?! On those papers, signed by a "superior officer," our last name was usually misspelled: Tardy with a y!

I know that it must have been hard (almost impossible!) for a military guy to correctly copy the name, but I noticed all my life that bad spelling wasn't just reserved for the military! No! Civil servants, doctors, teachers, journalists — they, too, would find it extremely difficult to correctly spell such a complicated name!

On the walls, there was a poster by the Communist Party with a dead little girl on it.

That little girl, dead from the bombs, hurt me deeply.

The alliance with Germany... A goddamn mess! Stalin and Hitler: two peas in a pod, isn't that nice? The communists weren't bothered by the German-Soviet non-aggression pact in '39! Not at all!! What's more, they didn't join the Resistance until after the Fritz invaded Russia — not before that, no! Shit! Shit! Shit!

Shush, René, you're being vulgar! The whole house can hear you, and your outbursts scare the boy!

It was always like that — my mother ended the conversation by saying: "Politics is unpleasant. I don't do politics!"

April 23, 1945, on the shores of the Danube, in Sigmaringen, former capital of "German France."

Eight months earlier, on August 20, 1944, Pétain had been arrested by the Germans and sent from Vichy to Sigmaringen. The "spiritual leader of France" is Hitler's hostage inside the walls of Hohenzollern castle. Along with him are Laval, the *Milice*, and a whole pack of collaborators on the lam.,, But the First Army arrives. The Marshal clears off — the Swiss are only 40 km away. On April 26th, he's delivered to the French authorities. On July 23, 1945, his trial begins. On August 14th, a national disgrace — he's sentenced to capital punishment. The conqueror of Verdun will be pardoned by de Gaulle. Imprisoned on the island of île d'Yeu, he dies on July 23, 1951, at the age of 95.

Elisabeth is unhappy. The French of the First Army entered the city yesterday and the door of the wine cellar, the family business, has already been forced open!

HOTEL LÖWEN

LÖWEN HOTEL LÖWEN

The young woman passes by the hotel where Louis-Ferdinand Céline stayed. The French doctor, who always dressed like a vagrant, had left Sigmaringen on March 22nd to go to Denmark, where he's been since the 27th with Lucette, his wife, and Bébert, his cat. Elisabeth couldn't care less about that — she heads to the castle, General Monsabert's HQ.

A very courteous man, the general receives her and listens to what she has to say. She speaks French well, which makes things easier. He agrees to assign Moroccan Spahis from his private guard to watch over the wine cellar and protect her as well. There have recently been many accounts of looting and rapes committed by the French troops.

Jean, a young sergeant, accompanies her. They never leave each other again. Michel will be their first child, born in 1947, in France, in deplorable conditions. The hospital nurses are particularly nasty toward the "Boche." Then in 1950, their second child, Sybille, enters the world in Sigmaringen.

Michel will also marry a German woman, Hildegard. I tell you this story because, much later, we become friends — Dominique and I will go with Hildegard and Michel to Czarne, Poland, to visit the site of *Stalag IIB*.*

The cellar. 60,000 liters of wine — no small amount!

*See the afterwords by Tardi and Dominique Grange in Volume 2.

In 1949, we went to Venzolasca, Corsica, with my grandparents, parents, "Boy," and Yvonne. That time, I joined them on the trip. I remember rides on the back of a donkey with my grandfather, small streams, and hazelnuts that we broke open on a flat rock with a large stone in the shade of the Spanish chestnut trees. Venzolasca was the hometown of my grandfather who fought in WWI. He had a heap of cousins: so many Dominiques (or "Doumés"), Antoines, Antoinettes, Maryses — and even a Pancrace... It was so hot there!

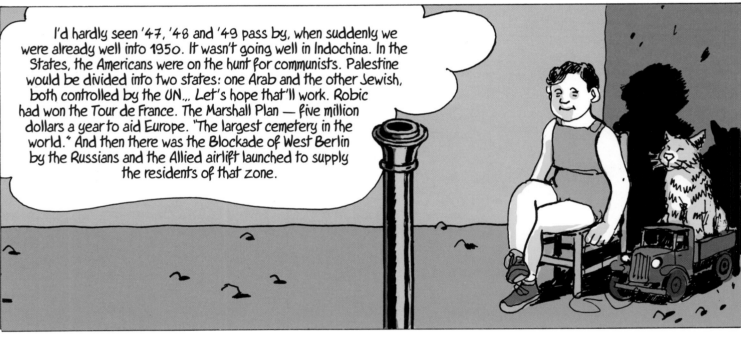

I'd hardly seen '47, '48 and '49 pass by, when suddenly we were already well into 1950. It wasn't going well in Indochina. In the States, the Americans were on the hunt for communists. Palestine would be divided into two states: one Arab and the other Jewish, both controlled by the UN... Let's hope that'll work. Robic had won the Tour de France. The Marshall Plan — five million dollars a year to aid Europe. "The largest cemetery in the world." And then there was the Blockade of West Berlin by the Russians and the Allied airlift launched to supply the residents of that zone.

My father is done working with wood! He's moved on to iron and copper. He creates a model of a steam engine.

CHOO! CHOO! CHOO!

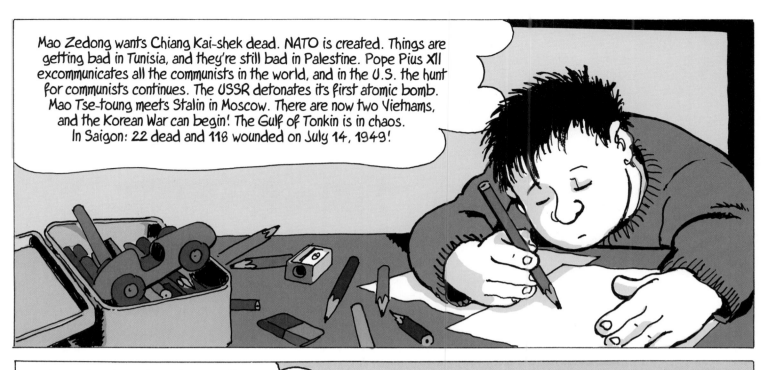

Mao Zedong wants Chiang Kai-shek dead. NATO is created. Things are getting bad in Tunisia, and they're still bad in Palestine. Pope Pius XII excommunicates all the communists in the world, and in the U.S. the hunt for communists continues. The USSR detonates its first atomic bomb. Mao Tse-toung meets Stalin in Moscow. There are now two Vietnams, and the Korean War can begin! The Gulf of Tonkin is in chaos. In Saigon: 22 dead and 118 wounded on July 14, 1949!

The Berlin Blockade ends. The Allies end the airlift after 277,264 supply drops. France didn't help much apart from a few pilots... We didn't have any planes!

The last model of the Roitelet flies well, but Fernand couldn't stop himself from equipping it with a more powerful motor. His son Roger has to do the test flights. Since Roger doesn't make it to the airfield on time, it's Fernand who takes to the air — and it's Fernand who dies behind the controls of the Roitelet on May 1, 1950.

The French National Railway builds the CC 7101, the fastest locomotive in the world, but it's electric... What a shame!

My father, who was on a renewable contract with the army, re-enlists for six months! It would have been wrong for him to deprive himself! They send him to Germany with the Occupation troops. He's to report to the military supply corps in Koblenz. He crosses the German border on February 12, 1951.

Koblenz.

What had he done during his stay in this city? Military things, of course, but what? I never asked him.

Three months later, on May 15th, supplied with a housing voucher, he shows up at 12 Römerstrasse, in Bad Ems, a charming city by the water, about 20 km from Koblenz. A few days later, my mother and I rejoin him.

We end up in a large, furnished apartment that we'll have to share with another soldier — the same rank and regiment as my father — and his wife and their son, Robert, a bit older than me.

The kitchen and the bathroom are shared. On our side, we have a dining room and a bedroom divided in two. I sleep in the smallest part. On the other side, the Lepages' — that was their name — the layout of rooms is identical.

The apartment felt immense to me, much bigger than our apartment on Serbia Road. There was a long hallway: a terrific playground for Robert and me!

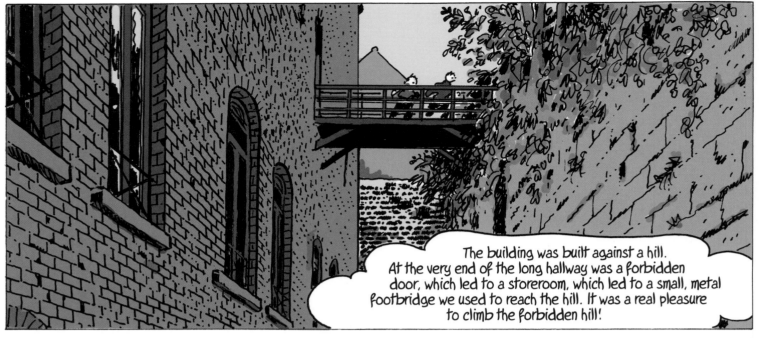

The building was built against a hill. At the very end of the long hallway was a forbidden door, which led to a storeroom, which led to a small, metal footbridge we used to reach the hill. It was a real pleasure to climb the forbidden hill!

Halfway up, above the roofs, on the other bank of the Lahn River, you could see to the right a little Orthodox church with its gilded onion domes.

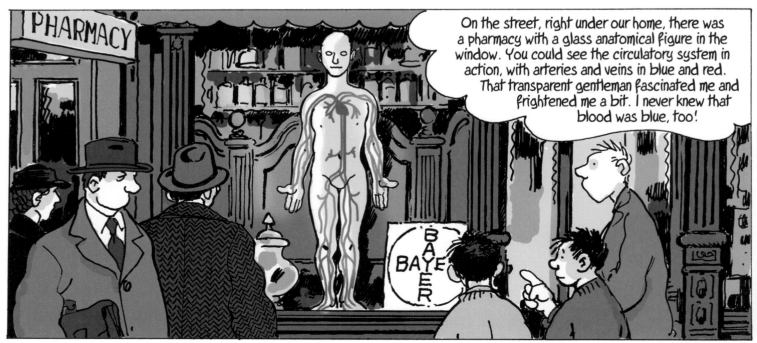

On the street, right under our home, there was a pharmacy with a glass anatomical figure in the window. You could see the circulatory system in action, with arteries and veins in blue and red. That transparent gentleman fascinated me and frightened me a bit. I never knew that blood was blue, too!

We had a German "governess" who walked us to school. She didn't like us and she crushed our hands in hers. She gripped very tightly and walked at full speed, dragging us along!

The German children in the "kindergartens" walked in a line, encircled by a rope that they all held onto. The rope formed a kind of protection zone, but it was totally symbolic. In effect, if one of them fell into a hole, they'd take the rest with them!

It was the start of my school years. If that's what school was like, I wasn't thrilled about it! So I enjoyed catching scarlet fever. A very nice German doctor came to see me. He said that I was contagious. Perfect — a few days of peace and quiet! Since I was quarantined, I fooled around without Robert. I played with my Schuco toys. I loved the metal boats... Unfortunately, they wouldn't let me in the tub. I cut out the Napoleonic soldiers printed on the inside of pasta boxes we bought at the store.

Bad Ems was a very cute, nice little spa town, practically intact, unlike Koblenz. Celebrities of all kinds — like Richard Wagner, Delacroix, Offenbach, Victor Hugo — had come to "take the waters." In July 1870, at the moment when it was thought he would take the Spanish crown, Leopold, Prince of Hohenzollern, and his cousin, King William I of Prussia, also "took the waters" there.

A Prussian on the Spanish throne!!! France feels threatened on its Pyrenean border. Napoleon III's Minister of Foreign Affairs, Agénor Alfred de Gramont, "the stupidest man in Europe" — "ein Rinvieh" (a bovine!), according to Chancellor Bismarck — wishes for a war with Prussia, just like Bismarck, the Iron Chancellor, wants one with France!

Leopold renounces the Spanish throne, but de Gramont demands that William I write a declaration with assurances for the future. The King of Prussia, very irritated, refuses. He can't do anything more, the affair is closed. The Kaiser returns to Berlin.

"It is important that we are attacked" — that's Bismarck's plan. So he drafts a provocation to France, the Ems Dispatch. In brief: "Go fuck yourself!" The French fall into the trap. "We'll enter Germany like a knife through butter!" To Berlin! To Berlin! On July 19th: War! (The Krupp company is thrilled!*) On January 28th, after the slaughter at the Battle of Sedan, France capitulates. Napoleon III is delivered to William I. He's immediately confined (in luxury) at Wilhelmshöhe Castle, near Cassel.

We live here!

Bad Ems was, in sum, quite a historic place!

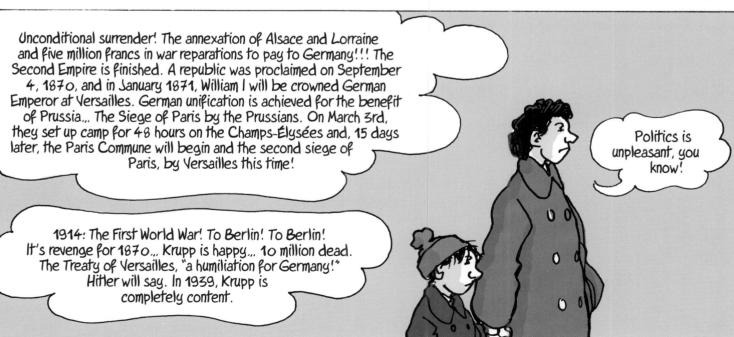

Unconditional surrender! The annexation of Alsace and Lorraine and five million francs in war reparations to pay to Germany!!! The Second Empire is finished. A republic was proclaimed on September 4, 1870, and in January 1871, William I will be crowned German Emperor at Versailles. German unification is achieved for the benefit of Prussia... The Siege of Paris by the Prussians. On March 3rd, they set up camp for 48 hours on the Champs-Élysées and, 15 days later, the Paris Commune will begin and the second siege of Paris, by Versailles this time!

1914: The First World War! To Berlin! To Berlin! It's revenge for 1870... Krupp is happy... 10 million dead. The Treaty of Versailles, "a humiliation for Germany!" Hitler will say. In 1939, Krupp is completely content.

Politics is unpleasant, you know!

*Krupp was an industrial producer for hundreds of years in Germany, known for it's production of artillery, ammunition, and other armaments for war.

On our side of the apartment, there was a library full of old leather-bound books. When we were alone, we tore out the flyleaves from those big, beautiful books and cut out airplanes.

From the balcony, we threw our airplanes into the street.

The shopkeeper below swept the sidewalk and threw them in the trash.

When he found out about the paper airplanes, my old man went crazy. His face went totally white and he picked me up. I was afraid he was going to throw me out the window. He shook me fiercely and then he stopped abruptly.

René!

He almost slapped Robert. Thankfully, he stopped himself in time! That would have caused a never-ending scene with his parents. After that, my father went to take a deep breath on the balcony.

You know your father has a temper... He shouts, he curses and says terrible things, but he doesn't mean it!

That sort of remark had a knack for exasperating him and, often, the shouts and ass-kicking would start up again even worse!

René! The Lepages can hear everything!

That would really set him off!

I don't give a shit about those idiots! Goddamn it!

Foul mouth!

My mother had a real knack for bringing something up at just the wrong moment!

One day, Robert and I climbed to the top of the hill behind the house. There we found an enormous, utterly sinister tower in the Greco-German style. The "Bismarck Tower!"

When I didn't have school, I drew. Robert fiddled around in his corner and I tried out my Faber-Castell colored pencils and Pelikan gouache paints.,, I heard my mother complaining to Mrs. Lepage. She grumbled about the damage I caused when I was born — her abdominal pains for which I was "responsible."

Robert and I were dressed up as cowboys, forced to wear identical satin costumes made by our mothers. It must have been for Mardi Gras or some other festival? They took a photo of us. There was a party with noisy kids, confetti, and lemonade. I would've much rather sat with a piece of paper in the company of my pencils.

My father went back to France a few times for a day or two. After one of these short trips, he brought back a few "illustrated magazines" for me, and a scale model of a Simca Aronde. The Aronde had just appeared on French streets. I thought it was beautiful, but he didn't buy one! A bit later, he bought a used Volkswagen.

We went to Koblenz often. The city had suffered enormously from the bombings, more than 80% of it had been destroyed... But now, in the ruins of the damaged neighborhoods the debris had been cleared, grass was growing again, and slowly things were being rebuilt — even the churches!

On the streets that were spared, stores were bursting with goods and I saw clearly that that upset my father. During these walks around town, he was dressed normally, in civvies, and he spoke a little German. Remnants from the *Stalag*, without a doubt...

Once, we found ourselves by the water.

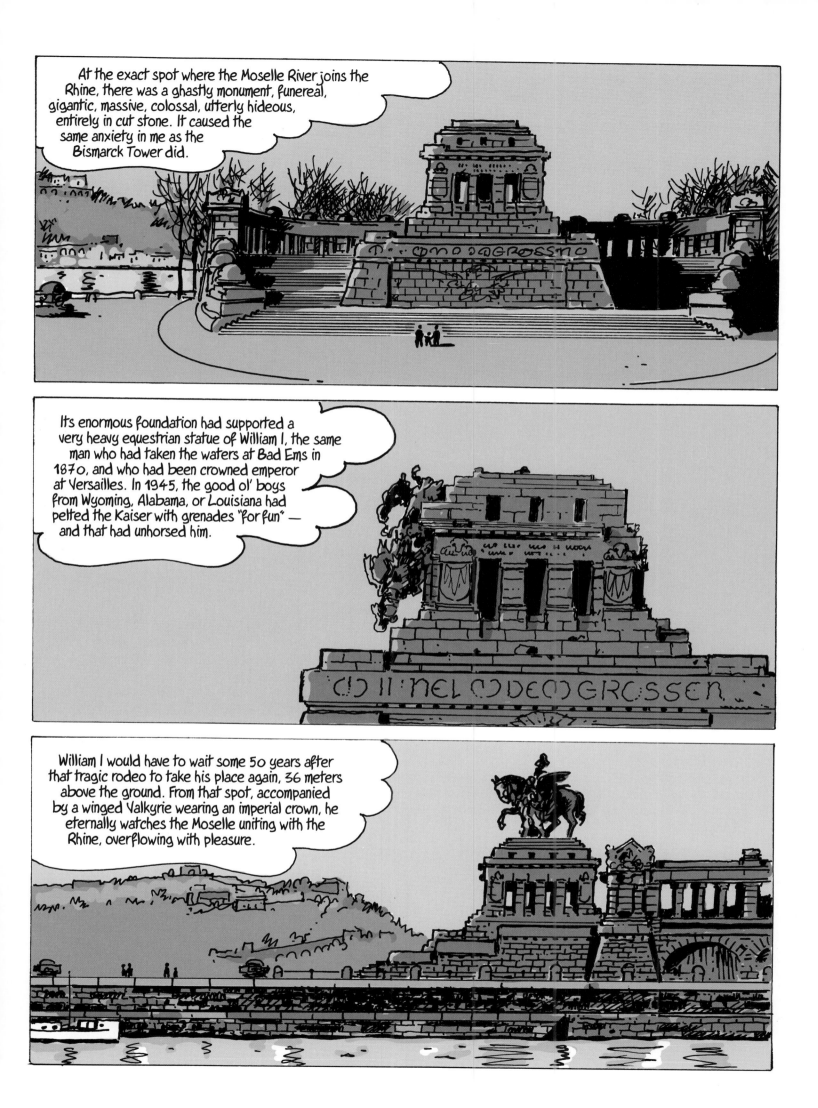

At the exact spot where the Moselle River joins the Rhine, there was a ghastly monument, funereal, gigantic, massive, colossal, utterly hideous, entirely in cut stone. It caused the same anxiety in me as the Bismarck Tower did.

Its enormous foundation had supported a very heavy equestrian statue of William I, the same man who had taken the waters at Bad Ems in 1870, and who had been crowned emperor at Versailles. In 1945, the good ol' boys from Wyoming, Alabama, or Louisiana had pelted the Kaiser with grenades "for fun" — and that had unhorsed him.

William I would have to wait some 50 years after that tragic rodeo to take his place again, 36 meters above the ground. From that spot, accompanied by a winged Valkyrie wearing an imperial crown, he eternally watches the Moselle uniting with the Rhine, overflowing with pleasure.

Sometimes, on the street, when the German pedestrians would see French military men coming, they'd walk straight at the soldiers to force them off the sidewalk and into the gutter.

Baden-Baden, a charming spa town and capital of the French Occupation Zone, had been, in '44, a stopover on the way to Sigmaringen for the Pétain loyalists coming from Vichy, another very stylish spa town.

The civil service in the French Occupation Zone is filled with thousands of collaborators, ex-senior officials of the Vichy. In some organizations, up to 80% — including the prefect, the deputy prefect, the corrupt policemen, and the low-ranking fanatical pigs who had, under Pétain, sent Jews and Resistance fighters to the camps!

Gaullists, communists, former Resistance fighters, and survivors of deportation stood shoulder-to-shoulder with those bastards, who, at de Gaulle's initiative in the '50s, will be exculpated and re-integrated into the administration with all their benefits, pay and retirement, paid retroactively — in "compensation" for their past as collaborators, I imagine!

A damn shame!

Even Papon?*

In Germany, the enemy is everywhere: in the city and the country — every man, woman, and child. Course of action: cool disdain. Authoritativeness (Germany must obey without question and without delay). No acts of violence, nor of rudeness. We're not Nazis. No relationships nor connections. No fists. No engaging in conversations of any kind. Those are, in no particular order, some of the orders from General de Lattre de Tassigny — future Marshal of France and Commander in Chief of the First French Army.

GENERAL DE LATTRE DE TASSIGNY SQUARE

Platzkommandanh

Soldat und

The First French Army was part of the Sixth United States Army Group under the command of Lieutenant-General Jacob L. Devers. De Lattre has no problem calling the army "Rhine and Danube," which everyone laughs at! De Lattre has no sense of his own ridiculousness, but he does have a taste for pomp and oversees his zone like an extravagant lord. Delusions of grandeur. He organizes farcical parades, supposedly to show the power of France, but it's just wasteful, an indulgent display, and it doesn't impress the starving Germans of the French Zone. By the way, they called him "*der ungekrönten könig*" (the uncrowned king), because they didn't understand what the French were doing there, since there were no French military victories to justify their presence!

*This is likely a reference to Maurice Papon who, serving as secretary general for the police in Bordeaux, was responsible for deporting over 1,600 French Jews to the Drancy internment camp from 1942-44.

BE SUSPICIOUS

Be suspicious... Somewhere in Germany are invisible paramilitary teams, hidden in the crowds, and they're watching you. Every German is a potential source of problems. Don't fraternize with any of them. The Germans are not our friends.

Germany's future is a rotten G.I. and a German whore! That's what you hear come out of ex-Wehrmacht mouths.

In the big cities, the Americans had organized all sorts of smuggling and started private clubs, dives, brothels, gambling dens... All until 1946, with complicit Germans and even Nazis who had managed to slip through the nets.

The "bra," two small triangles in West Germany: This is the French Occupation Zone, which was granted to France, proportionate to the role it played ("insignificant," says Stalin!) during the war at the invasion of Germany. In the French Occupation Zone, there are six million Germans, but no major city. Although Stuttgart had been taken by Leclerc, the Americans claimed the city. To pass from one triangle to the other, you had to go through the American sector with their authorization!

The French had a huge problem: The pathetic, defeated troops of 1940 became the "conquerors," but were fed, armed and clothed by the Americans! The Germans didn't give a damn about these post-war soldiers in the Yanks' provisions.

Here's what they'd say: "Take a handful of French, put an American uniform on their backs, sit them on a tank (also furnished by the Americans), wait for them to force their Moroccan and Senegalese soldiers to march behind the tank, and you'll see all the greatness of France!"

Baden-Baden is overpopulated. You can cross paths with 1,300 officers, including 800 colonels (most are civilians in novelty uniforms!). The occupying forces are settled in the hotels, the loveliest villas, and the finest commandeered apartments. They can bring their family and friends — so they make a buck off smuggling! Indemnification and recovery. Hadn't the Krauts set an example in France? It's revenge, and it's not pretty!

My father received a 10-day leave to go to Paris. At the border checkpoint, customs meticulously inspected all his bags... Plus, he had to change the headlight bulbs: white lights in Germany, yellow in France! We crossed the countryside, flooded by the Rhine as we approached from Alsace.

Papa, why did you buy a Hatler car?

Not Hatler! Hitler!

We arrived late at Uncle Désiré's house on Boulevard Barbès.

In number 75 on the 5th floor lived Aunt Laurence — Grandmother Tardi's sister — and Uncle Désiré. They were both actors.

You must be tired... A glass of port? Jacques, a mint water?

There's no doubt we feel better here! With the Boche, we don't feel at home.

HA! HA! HA! Good ol' Henriette!

My mother couldn't stop herself from saying something stupid!

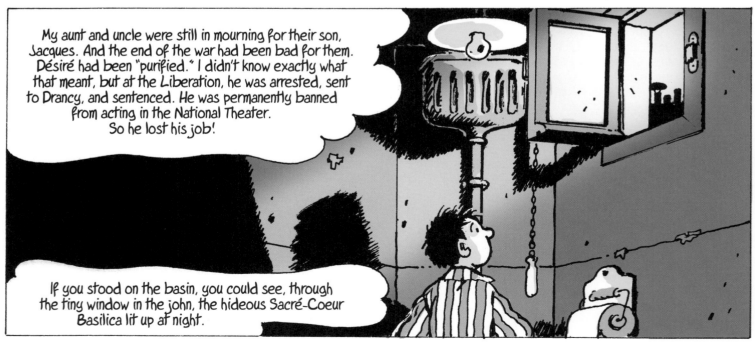

My aunt and uncle were still in mourning for their son, Jacques. And the end of the war had been bad for them. Désiré had been "purified." I didn't know exactly what that meant, but at the Liberation, he was arrested, sent to Drancy, and sentenced. He was permanently banned from acting in the National Theater.
So he lost his job!

If you stood on the basin, you could see, through the tiny window in the john, the hideous Sacré-Coeur Basilica lit up at night.

Since the end of the war, they had both been in a pickle, but continued to pretend they were rolling in dough. Aunt was rarely hired and Uncle showed off left and right. He dubbed American films. He did the cowboy voices.

They scraped by with small roles in educational matinées in suburban and small-town theaters. They played servants... took roles in Molière's "The Miser" and "The Imaginary Invalid"... gave Cyrano de Bergerac soliloquys... They were stuck with tours where they had to provide their own costume, sword, armor, and horse.

At the local theater in Valence I saw them perform for the first and last time. After the performance, they dragged me backstage. Aunt looked normal, but I didn't recognize Uncle with his wig... I was scared! He still gave me a toy plane that did loop-the-loops.

My mother had a doctor's appointment, so Aunt Laurence took me to the Vincennes Zoo. It was like a *Stalag* for animals.

Désiré had been seriously injured in Artois, in 1915. They hadn't sent him back to the front line, but he served as a guard in a POW camp for Germans.

Watching those miserable, starving prisoners, Désiré had concluded that the Boche were just like us: no better or worse. It came from a good place... But 20 years later, it started all over again. What a shame!

Let's stop fighting each other and come together to build the Europe of tomorrow... with the Nazi children of the guys he had seen behind barbed wire!? Désiré shared the Marshal's opinion. He supported the fight against the Bolsheviks and immigrants! He thought that there were already way too many people in theater... "We're all full up," he said!

It was a blast to go down Boulevard Barbès on the bus platform!

Maybe he had opened his mouth too much backstage? Maybe he had gone a step further? Maybe he had expressed his pro-Pétainist feelings too loudly? Maybe he had simply turned collaborator? My folks never knew. They never dared ask... He would've spun them a tale anyway!

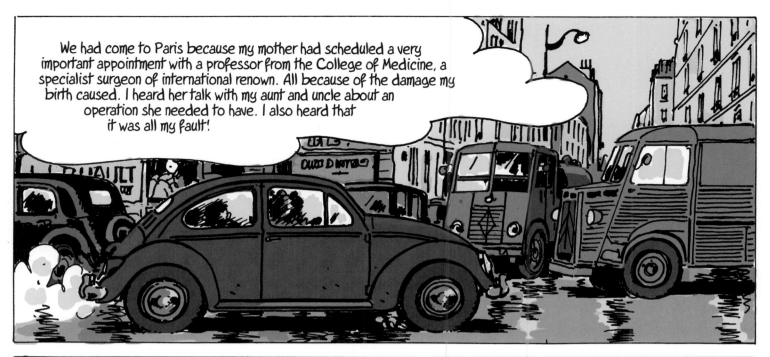

We had come to Paris because my mother had scheduled a very important appointment with a professor from the College of Medicine, a specialist surgeon of international renown. All because of the damage my birth caused. I heard her talk with my aunt and uncle about an operation she needed to have. I also heard that it was all my fault!

Back to Bad Ems.

In 1809, at the Battle of Wagram, General Lasalle, who commands a brigade of hussars comprised of the 5th and 7th Hussar Regiments, sees his brilliant career and his heroic charge brutally interrupted by an Austrian bullet in his head. Allegedly, he said: "A hussar still alive at 30 is a wastrel." Really!? He was 34, that idiot!

My old man is 36 when he goes to Fritzlar (in the American sector) to join a former *Luftwaffe* airbase, now the General Lasalle District, which, since August, has been home to the 5th Hussar regiment, re-established in Koblenz on April 1, 1951. He had been sent here for that "grand occasion."

DISTRICT
GENERAL . LASALLE

My mother is 35. I'm five when we leave Bad Ems for Fritzlar, 120 km farther northwest. We make the trip in a bottle-green Volkswagen.

It was from that very airbase in Fritzlar that bombers took off in September 1939 to support the invasion of Poland. For the whole duration of the war, the planes never returned to their departure point. Göring always had some destructive itch for them to scratch.

Fat Hermann would've hated knowing that this *Luftwaffe* base would one day welcome American troops with black soldiers... and French troops with the 3rd Algerian Regiment of Reconnaissance Spahis!

We're housed in an apartment on the first floor of a small building. Long and narrow, it's built on a sloped plot. There are two other identical buildings on this site. We live in the middle one. To this day, the Germans still call them the "French houses."

In winter, there was a lot of snow!

The population living in this sad place is entirely military. Did the *Luftwaffe* men live in these buildings? ... or the *Wehrmacht*? Here, too, we were assigned a German cleaning lady.

The "French area" wasn't very far from downtown Fritzlar. We'd take the bus there when my mother and I would go shopping. The façades of this stunning little city were timber-framed as far as the eye could see.

What's that statue? ... Looks like Joan of Arc!

It's Roland.

Mama, do y'see his peepee?

Shopping would sometimes take a while and I'd get bored. We'd stop at the tobacconist's. I liked that store and it's pleasant aroma. We'd go there to get the blends my father ordered for his pipe, which he stored in a jar with a piece of carrot inside to keep the tobacco fresh. We'd finish at the butcher. The butcher would always give me a sausage that I'd devour while we waited for the bus.

One day, my mother and I went to the barracks, because my papa got a medal!

He wasn't the only one. They gave medals to other soldiers, too. A general or colonel, it doesn't matter — an officer — pinned a trinket on the left side of each hero's greatcoat. There were a bunch of people standing at attention, the regimental fanfare, all the hullabaloo... And the Spahis with their big burnous cloaks... They were the handsomest! I was vaguely aware of how ridiculous the ceremony was, but everyone seemed to take it seriously. Puffed-up chests, proper expressions, side caps worn tight, gloved hands, and shoes shined just to wade through the mud. Much later, my old man will tell me: "I only wore my modest decorations once (on that day, in Fritzlar?). I never wore them again, not even on a ribbon." They ended up on his keychain!

In the pitch black of the early hours in winter, a bus driven by a reticent young German would come to pick us up at the curve behind our buildings to take us to a dreary, prefab school.

My school years were pathetic, but I'd get a prize for reading anyway, along with a book I didn't like.

When I wasn't drawing, I played with the other French kids. Behind the buildings was a slope that was great for sledding when it snowed. We had no contact with the neighborhood kids. I never had a German friend and I never learned a word of that "wretched" language.

We stuck to ourselves, we young French children, progenies of the glorious soldiers of that joke of an army.

As soon as a clock tower, a siren, or any sort of alarm sounded, my mother panicked. The Russians were coming!

We're about 60 km from the Soviet Zone.

KASSEL

FRITZLAR

You must understand that starting in 1949, the Occupation ends and so does the French Zone, which is integrated into the American and British side of Germany, part of NATO, led by Eisenhower. The Occupation's over! We are now "stationed" in Germany opposite the Russkies, and it's the COLD WAR! The Russians are 10 times stronger than the Americans, the British, and the French combined, and let's not forget that they also have the BOMB! There's a lot to be afraid of... Mama's afraid, not me!

A ton's happened since the end of the war... In the west, in September of '49, the FRG (Federal Republic of Germany) is created — and a month later, to the east, the GDR (German Democratic Republic) emerges. West and East Germany are staring each other down! The Americans bail out Germany with the Marshall Plan to aid populations "liberated" from Soviet totalitarianism. Its industrial recovery is urgent! ... Monetary reform: The Reichsmark is dead, long live the Deutschemark! It's an economic miracle! The Germans are even making little electric trains.

During this process of denazification, the Allies were utterly useless, and even more so in getting the country running again. Germany needed teachers, doctors, priests, all kinds of skilled workers, civil servants, cops, etc. But many of them had a murky past.

So in 1946, they put the Germans in control of their own denazification. There were courts under Allied control until 1951. It was easy, for a price, to find a witness ready to swear on his beloved children's lives that your behavior had been spotless from the start to the end of Adolf's reign. They were "soap witnesses" — they got your stains out!

Persil
für alle Wäsche

Your brother's going to marry Janine.

Basile! Married!

?

As Christmas drew near, Grandmother Archibald came to spend a week with us in Fritzlar. My father couldn't do thing to stop it. She slept in my room. We went on a walk in Bad Wildungen, a dozen kilometers from Fritzlar.

My grandmother was uncomfortable on the streets. She watched the elderly German men with hate in her eyes. It was embarrassing... Each time she was certain that she had just crossed paths with the man who had killed Collin — her first love — in 1916, somewhere on the front line.

Bad Wildungen, May 11, 1945. Eisenhower, surrounded by the officers of Bradley's 12th Army. Patton is sulking.

Patton   Eisenhower Bradley

After my grandmother left, on December 6th, St. Nicholas appeared in the stairs of our building. He wasn't alone. Old Man Whipper was with him. He rang the doorbells and the children came out to the corridor. "Have you been a good student?" "Have you been kind to your mother?" Old Man Whipper lashed the bad students on their calves (not too hard) before distributing gifts from his potato sack to the good children. It was the local custom and the good French people stuck to it. The cleaning lady's husband was the one with the whip!

One morning, at the bus stop, I almost killed a guy's dog. The dog would retrieve the snowballs we threw at him. I threw one on the hood of the bus — just before it stopped! The dog caught it in his mouth and he almost went under the wheels. I screamed my head off. The other kids doubled over laughing.

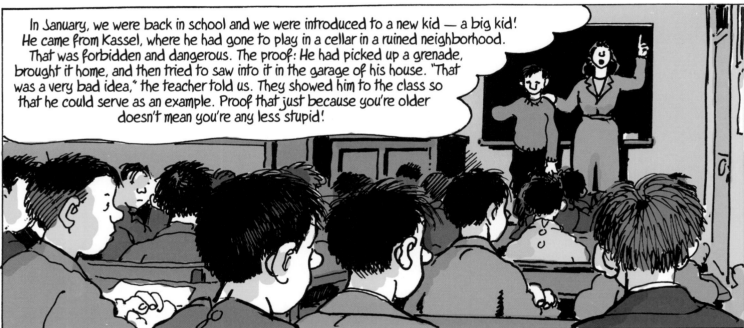

In January, we were back in school and we were introduced to a new kid — a big kid! He came from Kassel, where he had gone to play in a cellar in a ruined neighborhood. That was forbidden and dangerous. The proof: He had picked up a grenade, brought it home, and then tried to saw into it in the garage of his house. "That was a very bad idea," the teacher told us. They showed him to the class so that he could serve as an example. Proof that just because you're older doesn't mean you're any less stupid!

In Kassel, October 22, 1943, at 8:17 p.m, the sirens blare. 500 or so British planes are on the horizon.

At 8:49 p.m. a devastating bombardment begins and lasts for 30 minutes (or 22 minutes, depending on the source). 1,812 tons of bombs, including 400,000 incendiaries. The city is virtually demolished: 65% of the industrial buildings are hit or destroyed. They'll count around 10,000 dead. There were many POWs on the ground.

Thirty or so factories are ruined or damaged that Friday night... including Henschel, which makes locomotives, trucks, anti-aircraft guns, Tiger tanks. (6,000 POWs work in these factories.) Junker builds planes and Fieseler does, too, as well as the V1s. Most of the workers are foreign slaves. The Italian POWs will have to clear the streets and line up the bodies.

In a large park, at the top of a hill, there was an absolutely terrifying historical monument and a waterfall that cascaded into a pond. At the very top of the monument stood a colossal statue of Hercules. This pants-less fellow had a front-row seat to the Kassel bombardment! My father knew the Twelve Labors of Hercules by heart... These days I only remember the Augean stables, the Amazons, the Lernaean Hydra, and the Garden of the Hesperides... with it's golden apples.

Like in Koblenz, in the ruins behind the fences, grass was growing again. Whole districts had already been rebuilt. In the department stores, you could buy goods made by manufacturers who only yesterday were building assault tanks but had now switched to household appliances.

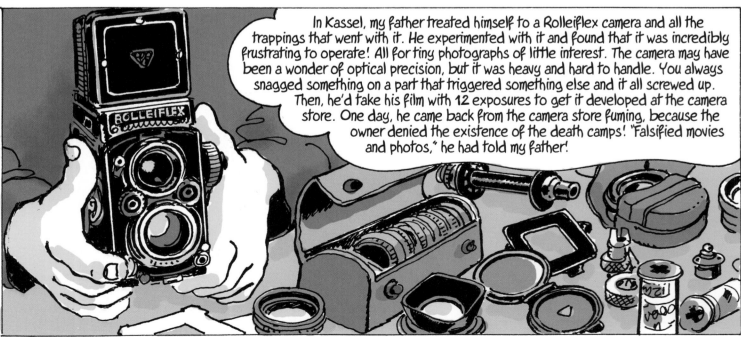

In Kassel, my father treated himself to a Rolleiflex camera and all the trappings that went with it. He experimented with it and found that it was incredibly frustrating to operate! All for tiny photographs of little interest. The camera may have been a wonder of optical precision, but it was heavy and hard to handle. You always snagged something on a part that triggered something else and it all screwed up. Then, he'd take his film with 12 exposures to get it developed at the camera store. One day, he came back from the camera store fuming, because the owner denied the existence of the death camps! "Falsified movies and photos," he had told my father!

My father sometimes left us alone for several days at a time for tank maneuvers. He said it was difficult to avoid intentional destruction. But some guys weren't burdened with scruples and passed over hedges, destroyed walls, gardens, small structures, and fruit trees with their tanks, since the Boche had destroyed everything back home!

Once in a while, we went to the Edersee Reservoir north of Fritzlar, to see the massive dam.

My father told me that a village had been flooded in the valley, and on full moon nights you could hear the bell-ringer's ghost tolling the church bells... and you could even see the top of the clock tower when the water level dropped.

May 16, 1943. Nineteen bombers (in three groups) that took off from England have just crossed the dunes of the Dutch coastline. Flying at a very low altitude, they've evaded the radars and the coastal artillery. They're now flying over the territory of the "Great Thousand-Year Reich."

They have three objectives: three dams — the Möhne Dam (the biggest), the Sorpe Dam, and the Edersee Dam! Their goal: Penetrate the dams to flood the valleys of the Ruhr, the Fulda, and the Weser, which contain numerous industrial facilities, including the steelworks and arms factories.

A conventional bombing would be ineffective. They have to penetrate the dam walls with precision. To do that, they'll release a spherical bomb over the surface of the water, which will bounce like a ping-pong ball all the way to the wall, sink, then explode at 10 meters deep — and pierce the wall!
The water pressure will do the rest.

To accomplish this, the bomber has to descend to 20 meters above the surface of the water, at a speed of 360 km/h, and drop a five ton bomb 550 meters from the target... All that by the light of the full moon — and while under fire from anti-aircraft guns!

Twenty meters! At that low height, the altimeters are useless, apparently... Two spotlights have been installed, one on the front and another at the rear of each bomber. The plane descends and when the two beams of light join to become a single circle on the water's surface, that's the right altitude! Twenty meters! Ingenious, isn't it? The Möhne and Edersee Dams are pierced, but the Sorpe Dam is only damaged.

There will be massive damage and up to a meter of water on the Luftwaffe airfield at Fritzlar! 1,200 victims, including many POWs and forced laborers. It will all be put back to normal quickly by slaves of the Third Reich! Eight bombers were brought down!

One day, we went to the circus in Kassel.

GROCK

GROCK

To this day, I remember Grock pushing his heavy grand piano closer to the stool that was too far away from the piano!!!

In the early '30s, another clown, a sinister one, came to see Grock — 13 times, apparently... Adolf Hitler! What an annoying fan!

Lederhosen... That's what these are called. Short leather pants with rhino horn buttons and an edelweiss on the suspenders. I even saw people on the street who wore them with coarse wool socks on their fat calves! That was my mother's idea! "They're stiff at first," she told me, "but you'll soon break them in, you'll see." ... Anyway, for the moment, they're impossible to walk in! My ass was in armor. I'd never dare to go play in the courtyard with the other kids — with these on, I'd be ridiculed and my buddies would laugh at me! I had to wear them once or twice around the house. I think that we gave it to the cleaning lady who had a son my age!

One Thursday afternoon, for whatever reason, Papa took me with him to the barracks. There were big trucks, hangars, tanks, and bustling soldiers. Doubtlessly, the soldiers were stirred by the glorious memory of the 5th Hussar Regiment. Inspired by the noble cause of their forefathers, the soldiers imagined themselves as defenders of the West, facing off against the Cossacks. The draftees, however, just wanted a drink!

At my father's request, two soldiers hoisted me onto a tank.

I was in total darkness. Light penetrated the turret only through slim vision slits. It was cluttered with levers, switches, handles, and other instruments that I was forbidden to touch, and it stank of gasoline. We drove a few hundred meters to the repair shop, because the tank had a mechanical problem.

My father was gone. I started to get scared surrounded by all the guys and the equipment. A young soldier with nothing else to do took my hand and we left to find him. Through corridors and up stairs, we came to the loft of a building. The young private seemed to know where he was going.

Papa was preoccupied. Along with another soldier, a captain, he had set up a train track set in the loft and they were playing like kids with my little Märklin train and one that belonged to the captain's kid. The Russkies could go ahead and stop by, the French Army was on the lookout!

And then, for my mother and me, that was the end of our heroic stationing in the Palatinate. Papa drove us in the Volkswagen to the Cologne train station, before making his way back to Fritzlar. We stopped in Paris and went to Uncle Désiré and Aunt Laurence's. My mother's operation date was set, and she would return to their home at the right time.

The next day, we departed for Valence. On the train, I got a bit of grit in my eye! We arrived at Mr. and Mrs. Chagrin's house on Serbia Road, dog-tired after a long trip!

With my father back in Fritzlar, we only had had some of our things sent ahead by movers. As for my mother, she had no intention of living in Germany ever again. She took a certain pleasure in showing her friends the refrigerator. They were still breaking blocks of ice for their prehistoric ice boxes made in France!

1952

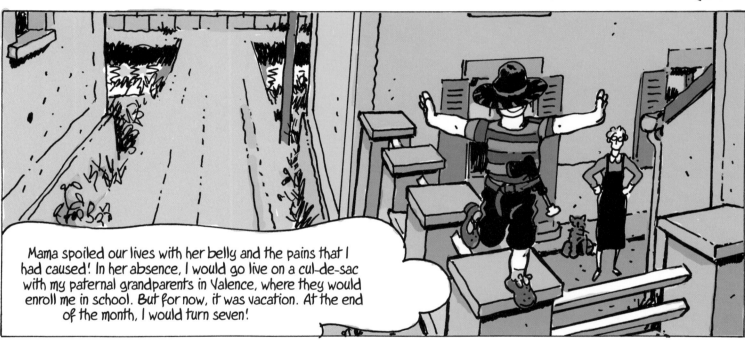

Mama spoiled our lives with her belly and the pains that I had caused! In her absence, I would go live on a cul-de-sac with my paternal grandparents in Valence, where they would enroll me in school. But for now, it was vacation. At the end of the month, I would turn seven!

And then, tragedy struck. Aunt Laurence threw herself from the 6th floor balcony of their apartment, and was crushed on the sidewalk of Boulevard Barbès. Désiré had cheated.

My mother went up to Paris to help my uncle with the funeral — which my father didn't like much — and to support him while he put on an act of profound grief.

While Mama was in the hospital, Désiré showed up without warning at my grandparents'. My grandmother didn't appreciate Désiré bursting in, since she considered him responsible for her sister Laurence's suicide.

Your wallet or your life!

Désiré walked in, held me tightly, cried his eyes out — such a talented actor! — and then gave me his wristwatch!

He prattled on about time passing so quickly, about the big hand and the little hand, and about life, which barely lasted longer than a good night's sleep — then the final bow! Right into the pine box! Barely born and already dead! He scared the piss out of me, that idiot, with his wailing... And then he added that one day we would go fishing together!

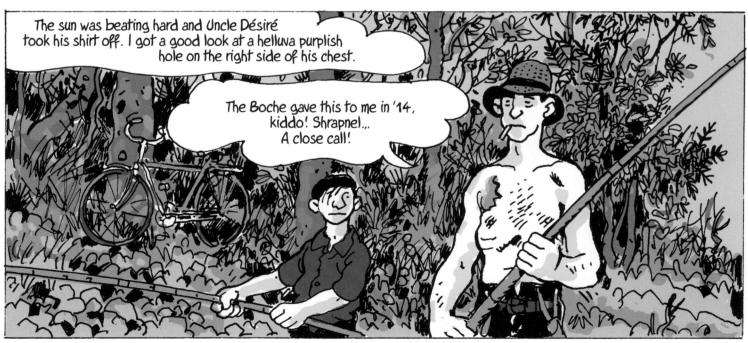

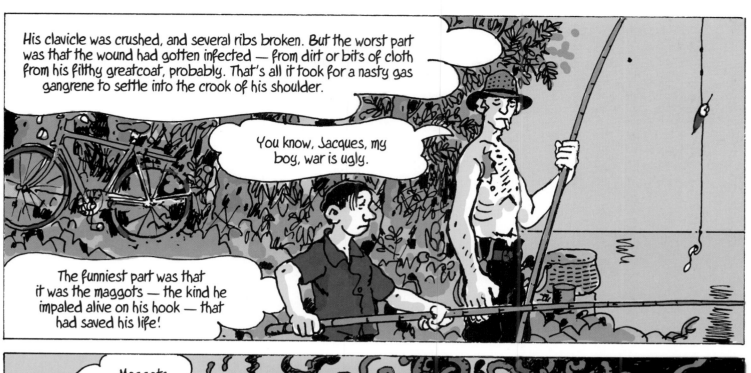

His clavicle was crushed, and several ribs broken. But the worst part was that the wound had gotten infected — from dirt or bits of cloth from his filthy greatcoat, probably. That's all it took for a nasty gas gangrene to settle into the crook of his shoulder.

You know, Jacques, my boy, war is ugly.

The funniest part was that it was the maggots — the kind he impaled alive on his hook — that had saved his life!

Maggots, worms, or earthworms?

MAGGOT. Limbless fly larva, such as blowflies, which deposit their eggs on decomposing matter.

Maggots had devoured the rotten flesh, which they were just wild about! That's how he got through it, thanks to the bandages covering his wound that teemed with disgusting, voracious maggots. It must've really tickled!

We returned to Pops's and Granny's house like a couple of idiots. We didn't bring back any lunkers... No fish fry! Plus, we fell into the water while crossing the little bridge over the canal. Uncle Désiré didn't have knack for riding a bicycle!

Doofus!

I relished the times when Grandmother Tardi and I went to town by following the banks of the little canal that flowed behind the house.

Although the canal was shallow, it made me anxious anyway, with the aquatic grasses undulating in the current like witches' hair, fat catfish, a few ducks, sluice gates, flooded washing places, small bridges, and a strong smell of rot! Watch out for polio!

There were narrow pathways that led to the canal. One day my grandmother chewed out a couple of youngsters smooching in a corner. She told them they were dirty, they were setting a bad example, they were perverts, they should take their hanky-panky somewhere else — and they weren't a pretty sight!

I didn't understand what could have justified such anger, nor what she meant by "bad example," and what did she mean by "hanky-panky"?? They scurried away in a flash!

Lili ("Lili" is what Pops called my grandmother Julia) didn't do the laundry in the canal washing places because, over time, the laundry would end up smelling like sludge. Instead she did it in our sink behind the house, right next to the john. Meanwhile, I'd be repelling cohorts of Roman legionnaires trying to seize the crapper! Lili could count on my extraordinary courage!

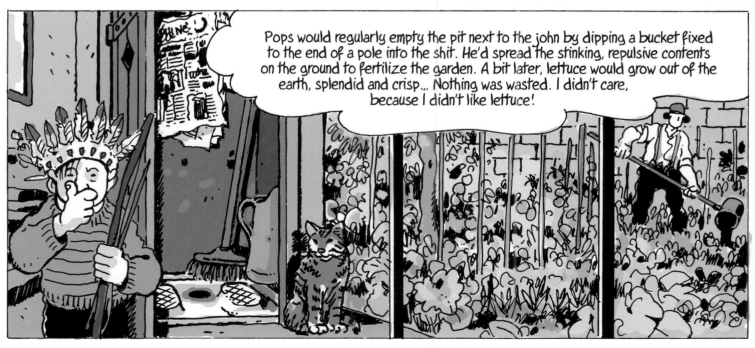

Pops would regularly empty the pit next to the john by dipping a bucket fixed to the end of a pole into the shit. He'd spread the stinking, repulsive contents on the ground to fertilize the garden. A bit later, lettuce would grow out of the earth, splendid and crisp... Nothing was wasted. I didn't care, because I didn't like lettuce!

Pops also regularly flooded his garden, and it was a real to-do... a game with the sluice gates! You'd open a gate that led to the canal, and — bam! — the water took off like a galloping racehorse into a channel flowing at the back of the garden, whose course we diverted so that the water inundated the vegetable garden, flooding the lettuce, tomatoes, parsley, and the godforsaken artichoke thistles that deserved to be sunk to the bottom of the ocean!

The hideous crickets crawled out of the pumps from their flooded tunnels and we were waiting for them at the exit to slice them in two with our spades!

In the summer, it was wonderful to dip your feet in the water. With a small shovel, I made rivers, islands, atolls, estuaries, deltas, archipelagos, and ports where warships were anchored. I'd carved these ships with my Opinel knife out of poor quality pieces of wood, and I liked them better than my Schuco metal boats. My marine riflemen, exhausted by tough battles the day before, could finally bivouac on hospitable shores — that is, until the seawalls cracked, drowning the poor guys!

My Pops is Corsican, like Napoleon. Whattabout yers?

In the garden I was a royal privateer, martian, Old Guard soldier, fur trader, dwarf, magician, harpooner of sperm whales in Solitude Bay, trapeze artist, cowboy, fighter pilot, deep-sea diver, trapper, Sioux chief. And I was Bayard the knight, d'Artagnan, Jean Valjean, Spartacus, Fanfan the swashbuckler, Surcouf the privateer, Mandrin the smuggler...
My cave wasn't far from here.

One day I was carefully advancing through the deep jungle of the cabbage patch — about to capture a black panther alive on behalf of the Pinder Circus* — and I made a discovery that would forever change the meaning of my existence!

Stuck between two cabbage leaves, I discovered some pieces of paper stained with brown smudges. Saturated by the rain, these scraps were pages from *The Free Dauphiné*, the local rag we used to wipe with and that Pops had spread in the garden with his bucket full of familial excrement. I suddenly understood why we often said that a newspaper was nothing more than a cabbage leaf — full of shit.

*An iconic, traditional circus that has operated in Paris for over 160 years.

In the yard, there was a chicken coop. Lili insisted that I swallow a hot egg every day. Apparently, it was good for your health. She pierced the egg at both ends with a sewing needle. The warm, gooey egg was totally nauseating... I wanted to barf.

For the cluckers to develop their shells, they needed to eat pebbles. So we took to the streets with a shopping bag and a coal shovel to salvage gravel from the gutter.

We stepped over the big hoses of the sewage pump truck, which smelled bad, as the workers looked on in amusement.

We also passed by the wine seller, who was drying his barrels in the sun. The smell wasn't bad.

While I waited for Mama to come home from the hospital and for Papa to get back from Germany, to my chagrin, I had to go to school. I didn't learn much in that school. It was Lili who taught me to read and also to write with a dip pen and, later, one with a much stiffer nib, like the ones she used at the Post Office.

I wasn't interested in school, but at recess we played marbles. I had a bag full of agates and terra cotta marbles (one agate was worth 10 clay marbles). In my bag, I also had jacks and a magnifying glass which I sometimes managed to light some bits of newspaper on fire with — against the rules!

Every day I had class, Lili gave me a snack for my 4 o'clock recess. A slice of bread with three pieces of dark chocolate or some Laughing Cow cheese and always a banana. I had to wolf it all down in a hurry, hiding in a corner of the playground so a big kid didn't swipe my snack.

I was jealous of my friend Norbert because of his rubber shoes! I'd never seen anything so terrific.

They were an impressive size, carefully molded with all the features: stitches, little holes, eyelets, with laces knotted perfectly on the top — all one piece of rubber and incredibly flexible!

At that time, I would've loved to have been as big as my buddy so I could own such cool shoes that didn't need to be laced up every morning! Really convenient. I've never seen shoes like that since then!

I'd eat lunch in the cafeteria at noon. I'd always stay for evening study so I could finish my homework and go home ASAP and play. The end of school was by far the best moment of the day.

The next year, I moved up to the big kids' class, so it annoyed me when, every now and then, my grandfather would come to get me after school. My buddies would make fun of me and call me a baby... We'd walk down Faventines Road to go home.

Along the way, we'd stop to see one of his friends, who was a shoemaker. They'd chitchat for a long time in his shop that smelled like glue, and I'd get bored. Pops was a shoemaker before the Great War.

Do you happen to know how to make rubber shoes?

He'd walk slowly, holding my hand. Sometimes, he'd have to sit, swallow a pill for his heart, and catch his breath. His lungs were in a sorry state because of the gas he'd breathed during the War of the Trenches. We'd eventually make it to the cul-de-sac.

The house was at the very end, not far from the canal and the little bridge where my uncle and I fell in the water.
I rarely went through the door.
I liked to climb
the wall.

The house wasn't very large, and it was damp due to the canal. Nevertheless, it was perfect for a retired couple. The ground floor had a kitchen and dining room.

The dining room was frigid. We never stepped foot in it. There was a Godin stove that was never lit, Lili's Singer sewing machine, and chromolithographs on the walls. The carpet was peeling because of the humidity and you had to walk on felt pads to keep the floor clean. The room smelled like wax and mold.

Most of the time, we stayed in the kitchen, where the floor was protected by a hideous linoleum and the table by an utterly banal red-and-white checkered wax tablecloth. In the winter, the coal stove heated the room nicely.

The radio had a place of honor on the sideboard with its big green eye staring implacably at us while it spoke endlessly of war.

In the yard there was the chicken coop and a long, narrow shed where my grandfather kept his old shoe repair supplies — out of nostalgia, probably — and his gardening tools. He also stored the coal there in an adjacent cubbyhole. The shed was built against the wall of the neighbor's house. The wall had a large, deep gash, a reminder of an aerial attack at the end of the war, it seems, after the landing in Provence*.

*The Allied invasion of southern France (aka Operation Dragoon) in August 15, 1944, is widely considered to have been crucial in hastening the Liberation of France.

We had a big tomcat, Pompon. One day — just like that — he hit the road... No forwarding address! So we adopted a female cat and named her Miss Pompon... obviously. This was the yard where I gave up my scooter to learn how to ride a bike without training wheels.

Thursdays, Lili made me do my homework. Sad days. Meanwhile, my grandfather snored over a book from the local library. They both borrowed books that they read all the way through after covering them with the same blue paper we used to protect books and notebooks for school.

ABRIDGED
LAROUSSE
ILLUSTRATED

I SOW WISDOM

5,800 ENGRAVINGS
130 PAINTINGS
120 MAPS

LAROUSSE BOOKS, PARIS

I had to learn multiplication tables by heart. Lili cared a lot about that! On the wax tablecloth, we had the *Abridged Larousse Illustrated Dictionary*. I didn't like The "I sow wisdom" Lady — she was ugly! But I enjoyed identifying the objects, animals, or things that all started with the same letter — like zebra, zero, zebu, Zouave — illustrated on the first page of each letter of the alphabet.

beef - balustrade - balance - bicycle...

I loved the history of France and Vercingetorix with his helmet, like on the cigarette packets. On the other hand, I hated that bastard Julius Caesar who gave Vercingetorix a beating at Alesia and imprisoned him for six years in Rome before beheading him!

Louis XI scared the crap out of me. After a hard day's work, he would go down to the basement in his castle and shoot the breeze with his imprisoned enemies, locked in iron cages or chained to heavy cannonballs — the so-called "King's chains." His depiction in the history books gave me the willies. I was afraid he was hiding under my bed, so every night, before going to sleep, I made sure he wasn't there!

As for Lili, she liked Napoleon best of all!!! Maybe because of my grandfather?

In front of the window, on the folding table Pops set up, I'd draw with my pencil and then add color. My Pelikan gouache paints — brought back from Germany — were almost used up. So, once I ran out, I used my colored pencils and went over the lines with a ballpoint pen.

Lili gave me advice since she used to draw, too, when she was young and went to her girls' school. One day, the teacher had put on her desk a bust of Marianne that used to be in the town hall, and Granny had knuckled down for several weeks on Marianne's Phrygian cap. It was drawn with charcoal, shaded with chamois cloth, and lightened with a kneaded eraser. Her "masterpiece" was thenceforth framed and put behind glass (charcoal is fragile) in the big upstairs room. It was like a photograph! I was impressed.

Conscript! ... How is it progressing? It's *mind-poggle-dee-ding** that drawing should require so much time... By Jove!

* Mind-boggling, I guess?

When I'm not playing with my lead gunners or my plastic Indians, and the garden is too gloomy because of the winter — I draw! I copy the cats from the Post Office calendar in their wicker baskets surrounded by wool balls... or I try to copy pictures out of my father's books, like *Camembert the Sapper* by Christophe.* It's crazy well-drawn and not easy to copy, so I tear up the paper and start over.

*Serialized between 1890 and 1896, this popular early comic strip featured the bumbling soldier Camembert, known to trip over his words.

When Lili visits one of her friends, they put me in a corner so I can sit down and draw. I always bring my notebook and a ballpoint pen with me because it's often difficult to find paper and a pencil at other people's houses! That way, I don't bother anyone and I'm a happy camper!

Lili talks to me a lot about Pops's war: The Seminal Catastrophe. The First World War... The Great War... The only real one! Not like my father's war — that he lost, for that matter! She showed me photos and also battle scenes beautifully drawn in the old editions of *Illustrated News*.

Not knowing what a catastrophe was, "The Seminal Cut-ass-trophy" made me imagine a war where all the soldiers had been cut up... cut up into slices like sausages.

Lili told me a terrifying story of what happened to my grandfather when he was in the "Great War." One night, after soup duty, he returns to the trench with two buddies. The Krauts hear them and shoot flares. (They're kind of like fireworks to see in the dark — that way you can see as well as in the daytime!) Bullets whistle all around them!

They throw themselves to the ground. The soup spills. Pops's two friends are killed right away!

Hands outstretched, Pops falls onto the belly of a rotting German corpse.

Like all French soldiers, his hands are all scraped up, and he's terrified he'll get an infection that could turn into unstoppable gangrene — and Pops is fond of his hands! He wants to wash them, but there's no running water on the battlefield!

He finally soaks his mitts in a shell hole filled with filthy, stagnant water.

Pops had lived through all that. I could hardly believe it. He had been injured several times and gassed, too. But the question that haunted me was: Had he killed any Krauts? He was rather calm. I never heard him raise his voice, and he was always gentle with Miss Pompon... War was for bad people, but Pops was in it, too, which bothered me. Had he killed the Krauts? Maybe just one? I never dared ask him. I was seven... We never spoke of it. Would he have answered? I'll never know. He didn't talk about his war. It seemed like Lili was the one who had been in the War of the Trenches. As for me, for a while, every night in my sleep I looked for water to wash my hands.

La *Boldoflorine*! La *Boldoflorine*!... The best herbal tea to get things moving!

On the radio, between ads, they had the news. They announced the death of a guy who some considered a god and others considered a vile bastard.

ARCHIBALD GROCERY

During a school break, they sent me to St. Marcel, to Grandmother Archibald's, to give Lili a bit of a break. I didn't like changing places; it was disorienting... It took me several days to get used to a totally different life at the grocery store. Luckily, I had my colored pencils with me and a brand new notebook.

SAPONITE
THE GOOD DETERGENT

CAFÉ HOTEL OF PROVENCE

Just across from the store, on the wall of the hotel, there was an ad for Saponite detergent. A representation of Marianne, like Lili's, was endorsing this "republican detergent" to a Napoleon-type guy and another character I didn't recognize.

At the shop there were now two cats — a Siamese and a Persian. Where did they come from? They feasted on the uncooked rice in sacks and my rubber suspenders, made from sock elastic. These two felines were almost feral. Only Grandmother could go near them.

Uncle Basile had his barbershop in the courtyard. He merrily cut his clients' hair and always enjoyed giving mine a snip. I liked the smell of the Hahn hair tonic, and I especially liked looking at the lights through the little blue bottles with flashes of purple, which had small white rubber stoppers and contained some kind of lotion...

Grandmother Archibad had bought a Citroën TUB van on credit for deliveries. Basile sometimes took me with him on his route to the remote farms. How could people live in the middle of nowhere, far from everything, in the flat, dull, wind-swept Rhône Valley?

We stopped in muddy, deserted farmyards. Basile honked and folks who weren't in the fields hurried right over. It smelled like manure. The dogs barked at us, they got a mean kick, and my uncle was offered a slug of red wine. Then we took off. I went two or three times... That was plenty!

My first cousin Michel was going on two, and he was in perfect health. As for me, my parents' faces grew hazier by the day. My father was still a soldier in Germany, and my mother had undergone a second operation and was resting in Paris at Uncle Désiré's, who was mourning Aunt Laurence in style! They warned me that her recovery would take time. She'd need lots of rest, and my presence would probably wear her out.

I didn't know yet that I was petting Gilda for the last time. In a few days, shortly after I returned to Valence, she would be killed by a hunter at the end of the yard behind the house!

If I could've filled that killer's balls with buckshot using an Ideal brand double-barreled shotgun ("The finest shotgun in the world," according to the first pages of the St. Étienne Arms catalog), I would've done it gladly!!! I cried a lot of tears for Gilda.

In winter, before going to bed, my grandmother would boil water on the coal stove for the brass hot water bottles. Then, in the stove, she'd heat a brick until white-hot for my bed. It should be said that the second floor rooms were freezing. They were unheated and, often before going up, you would turn on a little electric radiator... Plus, I had to piss in a chamber pot.

I remember the pleasant smell of the hot newspaper the brick was wrapped in, under a layer of towels.

In the room I slept in, there was a hand-colored photo of a soldier who wore the same uniform as my paternal grandfather. It was Henri-Maxime-Joseph Collin, my mother's father, who died in the trenches in 1916... He was 22! A grandfather I would never know... Had he killed any Krauts?

Berthe was still pregnant with my mother when Collin was killed. He had promised to marry her when he returned from the war. My mother was recognized as his daughter thanks to the testimony of two soldiers in his regiment, to whom Collin had mentioned the marriage that would take place once peace returned, as well as his unborn child... So she was a ward of the State! Berthe, a young mother, married Célestin Archibald, and Basile was an immediate result of her second marriage.

I spent hours swinging on the gate that guarded the stairs down to the cellar. I was a bit bored in this backwater town where there was nothing to see or do. In Valence, I used to go into town and sometimes to the movies with my other grandmother. But here, there was nothing.

Sometimes, Georges, the son of Jeanne and Dédé Robichon — the relatives that lived on the other side of town — came all the way to the shop by bicycle to do errands for his mother. He wheeled Michel and I around in the yard and to the end of the garden with the little cart they used to pick up packages from the train station. We didn't see Georges much. He was in school, at Romans. He was a sweet guy, gentle and calm. So in six years they'll ship him off to Algeria for the war!

In the countryside, they had no regard for the animals: Brutality and cruelty was their fate, before ending up in someone's stomach. I saw Berthe — nevertheless a very fine woman — break a rabbit's back with a sharp, precise strike with a club, then carve out an eye from the still-quivering animal with a razor-sharp kitchen knife in order to bleed it out. Its blood, gathered in a bowl, would be used for a stew.

Next, she butchered the poor rabbit, whose skin would be hung to dry on the line in the garden. There, it waited with other hides to be made, perhaps, into a coat! I wouldn't have enjoyed getting decked out in a coat made of animal skin! "Skins for sale! Skins for sale!"

The dining room was cold here, too, so we confined ourselves to the kitchen... Janine took care of Michel while Basile straightened up the cellar, Berthe prepared dinner, and I drew. After everyone went to bed, Berthe balanced the books for the day.

Cane, Shadow, and Bash!

For my best gal, an orange Fizz! For my best pal, a citrus Fizz!

Orange Fizz! Lemon Fizz! Fizz! Fizz! Fizz! Fizz!

"The Slackers Get Rich"
"The Slackers Escape"
"The Slackers and the Enchanting Perfume"
"The Slackers Go to Work"
"The Slackers Under the Sea"
"The Slackers at School"
"The Slackers in the Army"
"The Slackers' Buried Treasure"
"The Slackers' Big Win"

And Cane lets his buddies in on an idea he's been keeping under his hat.

So... whaddya thinka that?

Gee willikers!

THE SLACKERS

KICK OFF

Pellos, who drew *The Slackers*, was an ace at sketching the racers in the Tour de France with mountains looming in the background. Calvo drew disturbing forests with grotesque roots and branches and innocent little bunnies like the ones Grandma Archibald murdered in the garden. There was also *Bibi* by Pierre Lacroix and then *Zig and Flea* (and their penguin, Alfred) by Alain Saint-Ogan.

Ah ha! The thief isn't far!

SPLAT

I feel like I'm under attack!

An ape! What's it doing here?

Strange... Let's take a closer look!

Let's get outta here...

Hm! Not much farther to go. The Papuans must be around here... No... We're not done yet!

The Adventures of the Tramp, written and drawn by Forest, weren't like Chaplin's shorts they showed before the feature films with cowboys, but the drawings were stellar and there were always really pretty girls in these slapstick stories. I could never have imagined that in 23 years, Forest and I would make a comic together — the story of Arthur There, a Chaplin-esque caretaker in love!*

And if they're cheatin' the Comanche now, the ranches in Sundown Valley will be next!

There were also Westerns with Indians and cowboys like Hopalong Cassidy or Buck John. In these "illustrated stories," you didn't know who drew the interior art, but the covers were magnificent — like color photos, hand-painted. My favorite of these comics was *Prairie*, with Straight Arrow! When there was a bandit attack, Steve Adams, the owner of Broken Bow Ranch, would quickly put on a disguise in his secret cave in Sundown Valley and become Straight Arrow, the Comanche warrior and righter of wrongs, galloping on his horse, Fury — and go set things right!

I may be walking into a trap!

*Tardi's graphic novel collaboration with Jean-Claude Forest was released in English by Fantagraphics in 2009 as *You Are There*.

Right when I was starting to get comfortable in St. Marcel, Grandma Tardi came to get me and we took a bus back to Valence. Vacation was over and school awaited. Getting the flu would've been nice.

The busses parked in front of the savings bank, right next to the Champ-de-Mars Promenade, near the Peynet's Lovers Pavilion. I didn't understand what "Peynet's Lovers" meant. Who was Peynet and why did they love him so much?

We walked by the pharmacy. In one of the windows, there was a demon in green tights spitting fire, and it gave me the shivers.

Next, we went to the train station. We stopped at Nivon's Bakery to buy a Swiss cake, because that's where the best ones were, according to Lili... It was true! It was good for dunking in coffee with milk in the morning, before heading off to school. And a Swiss cake could last a long time. It was still good to eat, even dry, for days.

They say the cake was shaped like a Swiss Guard because of the pope that died in Valence... But it turns out that's not true. Anyway, I don't care about the pope!

We passed the train station where my old man, nine years ago, had disembarked on his return from Pomerania. And then we walked along the gratings beside the tracks. We went up the street to the tunnel that crossed the city and ended at the New Galleries department store.

It was across the street, on the other side of the tracks, that one day in 1943 my mother, unaware of the risks she was taking, had given out peaches to the parched deportees in a long convoy en route to the death camps.*

*Read more about Zette's exploits in Valence in Volume 1, pp. 155-156.

One we climbed out of the tunnel, we followed the dreary Alpes Street toward the house.

My throat hurts... I'm hot... I don't think I'll be able to go to school tomorrow.

We turned left and arrived at Faventines Road, at the spot where our canal rushed underground, continuing its course under the roads, even passing under the railroad. Lili and I traced the canal's path and crossed a bridge that spanned it.

And then we carried on to the little bridge where Uncle Désiré and I fell into the water, right at the end of the dead end, behind my grandparents' house.

I think you'll be able to go to school tomorrow.

Lili made me review my schoolwork and eat an early dinner. (Early to bed to be fresh as a daisy tomorrow morning!) I couldn't remember the eight times table and couldn't care less about verb conjugations. Tomorrow, back to school! I dreamt of a world without blackboards, where I'd be left alone — but I knew I was condemned to be cooped up in miserable classrooms for a long time.

THE DAUPHINE

Lili gave me a real earful when I told her that I never wanted to set foot in school ever again... "Shame on you! You don't appreciate the opportunity you have to learn to read and write! There are children who will have to get a job young and will never have the chance to learn! If you study hard in school, you'll be able to pick your career and get a better job than your father! Learn the eight times table!" Lili was a firm believer in public education!!

DING DING

THE D

Anyway, I got permission to read in bed. Five minutes, no more!

It wasn't just *The Slackers*.

I also loved to read and especially to look at the pictures in magazines like:

DYNAMIC TONY CYCLONE
TEMPEST
HARDY
ARDAN TIM THE BOLD
RED CANYON
VIGOR
HURRICANE
AVENTURES FILM TEX-BILL
METEOR SCIENCE FICTION
FULGOR

TAROO SON OF THE JUNGLE
N°8 MONTHLY TAROO GETS THE LAST WO...
36 PAGES

AUDAX BILL TORNADO

...sly, you're dangerous pal! ...dering how you managed ...undo the knots I tied with all the skill of an old sailor!

But Taroo, Son of the Jungle, and (in *Audax*) Bill Tornado, a cowboy and U.S. federal agent, were my favorite heroes. Both created (the writing and drawing) by Bob Dan (Robert Dansler), Taroo and Bill Tornado were the most daring of all the heroes in the comics published by Artima. On the back of each issue, one could look at the covers of all the titles on sale that month and dream.

Taroo coolly reached for an arrow and took aim at the lizard...

The marshal jumped and threw a powerful punch and hit the stranger in the gut, leaving him gasping for air.

Their rounds complete, Bill and David headed back to the U.S. Marshal camp to give their report.

Meteor!
Bill Tornado!
Ardan!
Tex Bill!
The Duke!
Garry!
Tony Cyclone!
Tim the Bold!
Fulgor!
Kiwi!
Sputnik!
Atom Kid!
Cocco Bill!
Hardy!
Buck John!
Pepito!
Bleck the Rock!
Red Canyon!
Vigor!
Hopalong Cassidy!
Victor the Pirate!
Iron Beak!

The day started well. In the first hour, the teacher, while passing by our desks inspecting our schoolbags, stumbled on my *Taroo*. It was the perfect occasion for him to get up on his soapbox and make a big show of it, the whole class laughing their butts off at my expense.

Well now, let's have a look at Mr. Tardi's very educational and enriching reading material! "Taroo, Son of the Jungle." Gosh, how inspiring! Let this be a lesson to the rest of you! Go right ahead and cultivate your mind with second-rate garbage like this! ... Straight to the trash! In the meantime, you've earned yourself 100 lines and one hour of detention! You'll stay after!

Jerk!

Once in a while, on Thursdays, when my grandmother visited one of her friends, we'd pass Serbia Road, which ran next to the Chagrins' house, where we had lived before going to Germany.

It wasn't much fun to stroll down the depressing streets in that neighborhood. Fortunately, some Thursdays we'd go see a movie downtown. Lili loved a good flick, and so did I. We got to choose from several theaters: the Rex, the Alhambra, the Palace, the Provence, the Mistral, and the Chalet.

TICKETS

COMING SOON

WILLIAM HOLDEN
ELEANOR PARKER
JOHN FORSYTHE

FORT BRAVO

with DEMAREST
with ANDERSON with BERGEN

We saw Eddie Constantine movies, which scared me, and Tarzan movies. I liked those ones! Tarzan was kind of like Taroo, who lived in the jungle, too, but Tarzan didn't wear an undershirt or boots or riding pants like Taroo did. All Tarzan had was torn-up underwear, a monkey (like Taroo), and a fiancée (unlike Taroo)! He let out a strange yell that I never could imitate.

EXIT

While watching a cowboy movie, I learned how the Mescalero Apaches, hidden behind boulders, had succeeded in perfecting their archery on the Union cavalrymen of Fort Bravo and the Southern refugee prisoners in a hole in the Arizona desert.

Too long. ① Too short. ② Bullseye! ③

Mescalero observer, directing the shot

Way to go, Mescaleros! They don't teach things like this in school!

One day, we watched a very long movie about Romans with their chariots, their fancy helmets with red brushes on the top, their muscular thighs, their skirts, their gladiator swords, and their slaves. The funniest guy in the movie was Emperor Nero, a complete nutcase.

Nero set Rome on fire. He sang off-key while watching the city burn, and then he accused the Christians of doing it. He imprisoned them, too, and sentenced them to be eaten alive by lions in an arena, but that didn't stop them from singing Mass... The Christians seemed to enjoy it!

But I liked pirate stories better.

On the radio, we listened to commercials for "The Bartissol Wine Man" or "The Bourjois Perfume with a J for joy" and a bunch of others... Songs like "The Little Dilly," "My Younger Years"*... the Pyrenees, the most beautiful mountains in France... "The Three Bells"... Edith Piaf... "Papa, Mama, the Maid and I." Jane Sourza and Raymond Souplex — "On the Bench!" There was also news, with names repeated over and over, like: René Coty (President of the Republic), Maurice Thorez, Jean Nohain, Tito, Franco, Gromyko, Louison Bobet, John Foster Dulles, Gina Lollobrigida, Eisenhower, Pius XII, Zhou Enlai, Adenauer, Chiang Kai-Shek, King Farouk, Winston Churchill, Marie Besnard, Gérard Philipe, Martine Carol... and weird things like the Supreme Soviet, the Iron Curtain, the sound barrier, "The Wages of Fear," the White House. They also talked about Fernandel, Sherpa Tenzing, McCarthy, Korea, Indochina, Iran, Palestine, Israel, kibbutz communities...

A FILM BY
JULIEN DUVIVIER
FERNANDEL
GINO CERVI

THE LITTLE WORLD OF
DON CAMILLO

And then one day, after school, a big kid let me look at his magazine — two minutes, no more! — and I flipped through it for the first time. It wasn't like Taroo. It was much better and almost all in color, with all sorts of different stories to read... serious ones and funny ones. Plus, this one came out every Friday! That's how I met Captain Haddock!

The next Friday, my grandmother agreed to buy me an issue of Tintin magazine. Since she thought it was much better than Taroo, Audax, Vigor, and Fulgor, she bought it for me every Friday. I spent much more time looking at the pictures in the magazine than I did reading the stories stuffed with words — the drawings were enough for me! Tintin walked on the moon, of course, but I liked Captain Haddock far more. Their rocket made me think of the wax tablecloth on the kitchen table where I sat to copy certain pictures.

*"My Younger Years" ("Mes Jeunes Années") is a nostalgic song about childhood memories of the Pyrenees composed by Charles Trenet in 1948.

During this time, Marsupilami and I crossed paths in *Spirou* magazine, at the exact moment when he was beating up an animal trainer in a small circus that made me think of the Kassel circus where I saw Grock, the clown.

HUBBA! HUBBA!

OPE!

KSS SS

HOP

HOP

This is it! One good crack of the whip...

HUBBA!

HA HA HA

CLAP HA HA CLAP CLAP HA HA

HA HA

BRAVO

ZWIPPP

OPE!

HA HA HA

BRAVO

CLAP CLAP HA HA CLAP CLAP HA HA

I would never have dreamed that 45 years later, I'd be asked to draw the cover of a weekly TV magazine to pay homage to Franquin, the amazing artist of Marsupilami and Spirou, who had just passed away.

Lili always took me with her when she went shopping in town.

On Grand Street, we walked past the House of Heads. Before becoming the famous Napoleon Bonaparte, Napoleon had lived just across the street from this house, in 1785, while he was still just a lieutenant in an artillery regiment. Not far was Clerics Square, where the legendary highwayman Louis Mandrin had been sentenced to being broken by the Wheel 30 years earlier — with 6,000 spectators watching! And thus the sinister Valence court made him into a hero!

One day, at the bottom of the drawer on the sewing machine, among the bobbins, I discovered a photograph. It depicted a seashore — which sea? — and on the rocks, my grandfather, my grandmother, Aunt Laurence, my father, and a sickly kid. The kid was Jacques, Aunt Laurence and Uncle Désiré's son. My old man's first cousin who died of polio at eight... same age as I was. In memory of him, I had been given his name — a dead child's name!

Actually, I'm seven and a half.

We just received a letter from your father. Your parents will be back soon. Your mother is doing better but she'll wait at Uncle Désiré's until René returns from Germany. They'll both soon be on their way back. Are you happy? Did you do your homework? Sit up straight!

SCHOOL FOR BOYS

My parents were about to come back, and I didn't really care. Where were we going to live? That detail especially nagged at me. I wasn't thrilled about going to the store in St. Marcel. I preferred my grandparents' house in Valence. I was worried... Fortunately, when school got out, my pal Norbert and I compared the virtues of the heroes from our favorite comic books. I found out that's what's what they called the stories we read in our magazines — comics.

My parents were finally here!
My father parked his car in front of the door and
honked to signal their triumphant return.

We rushed out!
Everyone hugged and
kissed — an endless maelstrom of emotion!

Mama, wearing the lousiest, ugliest hat, pressed me tightly
against her ample chest and I almost died from suffocation.
After that, she explained to me, with tears in her eyes and a sob in
her voice, that she had undergone two operations and suffered a
great deal — and it was all my fault. My birth had been difficult.
Since I hadn't wanted to come out, they had had to use
forceps. I had torn everything up on my way out!

By the way, she said to me, the little
scar I had on my left eyebrow was
made by the forceps!

She couldn't have any more children; and she had longed for a
little girl instead of a boy, because girls are kinder to their
mother... I listened unflinchingly to all that crap — and it
was only just beginning!

My father chatted with Pops to one side.
Lili said nothing. We snacked in the kitchen.

Mama told me that her and Papa would go live for a bit in St. Marcel, above Grandma Archibald's store. And then they talked about some other things. Mama complained about her fate, her belly, her suffering... After finishing the Swiss cake, everyone rose from the table.

Goodbye... more emotional hugs and kisses...
See you soon! Papa sulked. Then they left, reversing back out of the dead end.
It was time for them to hit the road. It was as if we were strangers.

They had decided that I would stay here until the end of the school year. After that, they would come get me. But for the moment, I should keep up with my homework and learn my lessons.

It's me, Taroo, Son of the jungle!

Later on, I understood why my father was unhappy. He had just finally left the army — it was time! — and he had a plan. But to follow it through, he needed cash. He had imagined borrowing the money from his father, who had some set aside, but Papa's pitch hadn't excited Pops. Pops didn't believe he'd ever see his dough again! For him, there was nothing more to life than serving the public... The civil service was the only true thing.

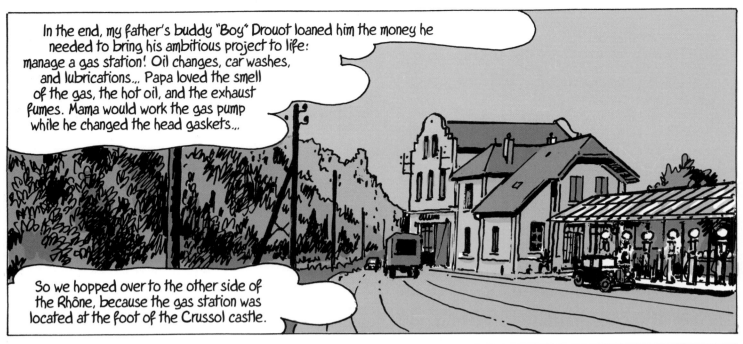

In the end, my father's buddy "Boy" Drouot loaned him the money he needed to bring his ambitious project to life: manage a gas station! Oil changes, car washes, and lubrications... Papa loved the smell of the gas, the hot oil, and the exhaust fumes. Mama would work the gas pump while he changed the head gaskets...

So we hopped over to the other side of the Rhône, because the gas station was located at the foot of the Crussol castle.

Papa changed cars, but he bought one smaller and plainer than the Aronde.

At the station, there were six gas pumps. On the ground floor of the building was a restaurant with a bar. Mama, in addition to pumping gas, took care of the bar, cooked food, and served the travelers, with help from Gilberte, a local girl.

It had been a motel, with four rooms on the second floor, but the former manager had quickly transformed it into a "no-tell" motel. What did that mean? The waitress at the time went up to the rooms. The police had shut it down right before our arrival.

On the weekend, the bar was hopping. Some doofuses pulled on the bow of Gilberte's little white apron and everyone laughed. But when I did the same thing, I got smacked upside the head.

One day, my father asked me to go find something in the garage and, there, I saw Gilberte on a pile of coal. She was lying underneath a truck driver. They had thrown a blanket on the lumps of coal and were moving rhythmically together. I quickly shut the door!

With the bar, the truck drivers, and the waitresses, my mother said that this was no place for me. That's when Roger, who had just let go of his repair shop in Romans, came to take over from my parents at the station. Before leaving, we had some time to mess around in the countryside with Max, my cousin, three years younger than me.

That didn't last long. One night we were robbed. We didn't hear a thing. In the safe on the ground floor, the thieves found the receipts for the day and the P08, the Lüneburg pistol, which they swiped. The thieves were quickly busted. The pistol hadn't been fired... thankfully!

Papa almost got into trouble. He hadn't had the right to own such a weapon. "But it's a prize of war!" he said. "Doesn't matter!" and the cop kept the gun for himself — for his collection, surely! I was sure Papa was going to hit the dirty thief!

PAPA!

RENÉ!

After voluntarily enlisting in 1935 and serving 18 years in the army, including five in captivity, Papa crossed the Franco-German border on April 30, 1953. They wanted to send him to Indochina, but he no longer wanted to play the dead hero for France! Moreover, what the French were doing in our "beautiful colonies" repulsed him and he said that we were absolute shitheads! So he didn't renew his contract with the French Army!

RF

END

TARDI

Just before summer vacation, I said goodbye to my pal Norbert. I gave him my magazines: the *Tintins*, the *Spirous*, and the *Audaxes*. I only kept my *Taroos*. I had the idea that we could trade my comic books for his rubber shoes — but I hadn't dared ask.

Thank you to Dominique and my cat Pipô, who helped me bear the heavy burden of memory during this entire journey, from Stalag IIB to Fritzlar.

—Tardi

AFTER THE WAR... FROM KOBLENZ TO VALENCE

TARDI + DOMINIQUE GRANGE

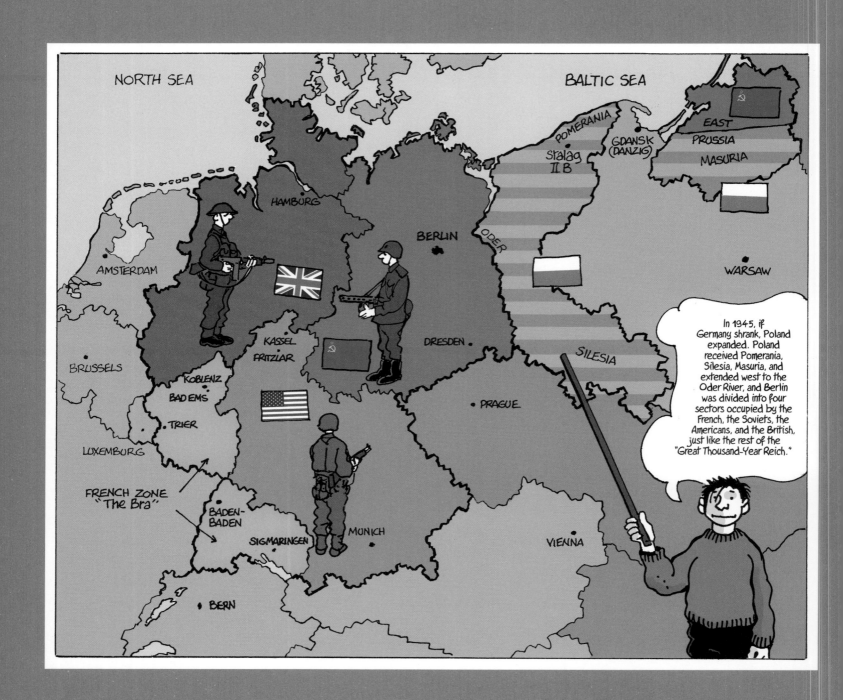

In 1945, if Germany shrank, Poland expanded. Poland received Pomerania, Silesia, Masuria, and extended west to the Oder River, and Berlin was divided into four sectors occupied by the French, the Soviets, the Americans, and the British, just like the rest of the "Great Thousand-Year Reich."

BAD EMS... The corridor is not as long and much smaller than I remember. At the far end, behind the door on the third floor that opens onto the dizzying drop of the backyard, the narrow metal footbridge is gone. Since then, things have changed, of course, but you can still access the hill behind the building and climb above the roof-level. On the right, when you look toward the opposite bank of the river, you can still spot the Orthodox church, with its gilded roofs shaped like onions, glittering in the sun.

"This is the bathroom here, isn't it?" Michel translates my question for Mrs. Bermal Ikiyek, the new owner of the apartment. She opens the door... It's still the bathroom, but the tub is sitting in a different direction! "You're right," the lady confirms with a little smile, "the bathroom was reconfigured!" I would've liked to open other doors... We shared that apartment with another officer the same rank as my old man, his wife, and their son, Robert. The kitchen and the bathroom were communal. The other rooms had been divided — everyone got their own space!

At the moment, we're drinking coffee in the family room with Mrs. Ikiyek and her children, Hildegard, and Dominique. A huge TV mounted on the wall broadcasts a soccer game, subtitled in Turkish. I explain that, at the time — Michel translates! — this room was divided in two by a partition that defined a room where I had spent some time "in quarantine"... scarlet fever! That must have been in 1951. We go out on the balcony. This is where Robert, whom I had befriended, and I threw our airplanes cut out from the flyleaves of the beautiful old works that filled the library (the apartment was furnished). The pharmacist on the ground floor swept up our planes, crash landed on the sidewalk. He had to have seen the swastikas we had drawn on the wings of these planes that flew badly. The balcony still overlooks the roofs of the casino and the spas of Bad Ems, where William I, in this very place, took the waters in 1870! On the same bank, at the top of the hill, wasn't there a Bismarck Tower? I recalled that you accessed it via a wooden cable car.

We met a German historian in Luxemburg during a debate about World War I following a performance of our show, *Goddamn This War!* — I read my script and Dominique sang, accompanied by the music group Accordzéâm (my daughter Rachel handled the editing and projection of drawings from the book.) Her name was Susanne Brandt and, as soon as she heard the name Fritzlar, advised us to contact Mr. Preuss. Once again, Michel Gosselin was tasked with reaching out. Mrs. Brandt pointed Michel toward Mr. Jürgen Preuss and Mr. Hans Feih — a Luftwaffe lieutenant colonel and retired colonel, respectively — as well as toward Mr. Clemens Lohmann, the Fritzlar archivist, to schedule a meeting with each of them.

LEFT
Dominique Grange, Mrs. Ikiyek, and Michel Gosselin on the famous balcony where we threw our planes!

It's true that *Oberstleutnant* Preuss is an excellent, knowledgeable guide. We walked around the site of the old aerial base, occupied first by the Americans in 1945, next by the French who turned it into the General Lasalle District, then the 5th Hussar regiment came, and finally it was turned over to the German Air Force. I brought photographs of the places we were visiting, taken by my father. Mr. Preuss explained everything to us, but we didn't have authorization to enter the interior of the premises. We went alongside the runways, near the old control tower where the bombers took off in 1939, toward Poland!

Fritzlar! To find yourself in city streets is suddenly somehow reassuring! Fritzlar, a charming little town with so many timber-framed buildings! And Roland, in his fountain, jumps out to me immediately — I had forgotten him. Suddenly, the memories of wandering in these streets with my mother come back to me. In the city archives, Mr. Lohmann — accompanied by his spouse, who teaches French — waits for us. Hundreds of photographs in black and white of the French presence in the city are presented to us in small, neat stacks on a large table. How did they get here? Were they official photographs? Mr. Preuss explains that a photographer had set up a crude hut near the entrance of the barracks where he developed photos of the French! I look at the photos of all sizes a bit too quickly... There are so many! You would need to spend hours with them. I recognized faces and then, suddenly, Dominique spots me in a shot, apparently taken during a school party in the mess hall: "Look here! Look, it's you — I'm sure of it!"

"What did you think of the French?" (Mr. Preuss is two years younger than me.)

"They were here to help. The Russians were 60 kilometers from Fritzlar. It was the Cold War. It's obvious that the 5th Hussar regiment and its staff of Algerian Spahis, with their American Chaffee tanks (later, they'll be equipped with AMXes), would have pushed back the Red Army all by themselves!" By the way, he asked, did I have German friends at the time? No, I said, none! No contact between us and the population. I didn't learn German either!

We went outside the city to see the buildings we had lived in. There, too, I recalled fights, sledding, snowballs, and games we played around these dreary structures.

Bad Wildungen, some 10 kilometers away... same type of city as Fritzlar, but with large hotels around. I see the sloping Grand Street again, in winter... like today. We go all the way to the Edersee. The dam hasn't moved, the repaired breach clearly visible.

Kassel... Its monumental waterfall with Hercules at the top. And the unforgettable clown, Grock! The large, industrial city had been bombed extensively. At the time, it was being rebuilt, but the toy stores were packed with little metal Schuco cars and boats, as well as Märklin trains. And for drawing, there were Faber-Castell colored pencils and Pelikan gouache paints in trays. I hadn't forgotten the pleasant smell of UHU glue sticks (UHU sounds like an owl's hoot — of course there was still an owl on the tubes!).

Koblenz... the enormous monument at the edge of the water! William and his Percheron horse still hadn't gotten their base back!

Frankfurt... Of course, there may have been many other memories to conjure up here, but it ran the risk of being boring.

1952–1953: Return to France. There was Taroo, Son of the Jungle, Bill Tornado, and so many others... The birth of a vocation, frantically fought against by narrow-minded teachers who, obsessed with the idea of protecting my future, tore up my "illustrated magazines" in front of all the delighted students!

—Tardi

Well, the circle is complete... At least it seems to be, since René, torn from his native land in Drôme by the war, is finally headed back to Valence. After five years of captivity and five months of an endless march through a devastated Germany, he survived, like most of his comrades, the cold, the hunger, and the physical exhaustion, from East Pomerania to the border of his beloved birthland — which, evidently, had nothing planned for the return of the hundreds of thousands of prisoners of war flocking from Germany, full of hopes of finally attaining what they had dreamed over the course of nearly 2,000 sleepless nights in the camp beds! No, the prisoners of war were not welcomed home, for they were held responsible for France's defeat by the German invaders in May/June 1940. The suffering endured during their captive years in Germany elicited neither interest, nor compassion, nor, most importantly, the slightest support in helping the men regain a "normal" life within their families or society.

René and Zette married before the war, in 1937. In 1946, after the father's return, a little boy named Jacques made his appearance. But there was no work. So, to feed his family, René remained in the army, waiting to one day find something better. I am trying to imagine what a shock it must have been, his head still full of the orders bellowed constantly by the *Posten* (the guards at the *Stalag*) — AUFSTEHEN! (Up!), SCHNELL! (Quickly!), LOS! (Go!), RAUS! (Out!), ARBEITEN! (Work!) — what a shock to learn that he would be sent back to where he had just lost five years of his youth, of his life: Germany! I am trying to imagine what must have gone through his mind when the train that brought him back there crossed the border... From that point, he would be part of the occupation troops whose mission was one of observation, surveillance, denazification, but not, at this stage, reconciliation with a population whose language he hadn't learned, except the shouts mentioned above!

He had arrived at *Stalag* IIB in May 1940 and had never since come to terms with the humiliation of defeat. Also, even if, in 1951, you could think that he was returning to Germany as a victor — that is, with the Allied troops — he must have felt profoundly the absurdity of such a reversal of his situation, mixed with the anguish of having to build a peaceful family life in a country where he had known only suffering and depravation of freedom, a country that he had every reason to hate down to his bones during his five years of captivity!

The little boy named Jacques is only four at the beginning of 1951, when René leaves Valence for Bad Ems. Zette joins René a bit later to move into the apartment on Römer Street. That's where we decided to go in 2017, to try to find these places that had sheltered Tardi in his early childhood, much too young to grasp the complexity of his father's life. Suddenly, there's the city, the river, the Orthodox church, the setting he described to me, and finally, Römer Street, which Michel Gosselin (our French-German friend) marked on a map after a historian in Bad Ems, Wilfried Dieterichs, identified the apartment in December 2013. That same year, Michel and Hildegard had accompanied us to reconstruct René's path home through Germany (Volume 2). We're searching for the address number... Here it is! I look at Jacques, his emotion palpable — I think his heart is thumping as he climbs up the stairs... He becomes agitated, and then, suddenly, he says, "Yes, this is it. I remember the banister on the landing there. Yes, I seem to recognize it..." Michel calls the owners of the apartment, who agree to our visit, and, quickly, the door opens and there's

ABOVE

Clockwise from top left:
Grandmother Archibald,
Grandmother Tardi,
René Tardi, Zette.

a woman and two children who welcome us with a smile. Obviously only Michel and Hildegard will be able to chat with them, but our loyal interpreter scrupulously translates every question that comes to mind, as well as the lady's explanations. We visit the main rooms. Tardi's face betrays no emotion. I see him slip into every corner, noticing details here and there, on the ceiling or elsewhere, a door or a dividing wall "which wasn't here, I'm sure!", the corridor that was his playground and which was, in his memories, "much longer." The bathroom was modified as well. Redone several times perhaps; after all this time, who knows? But the "tub definitely wasn't there... it went the other way." He's excited. It feels like I'm watching the puzzle pieces in his mind gradually coming together, reconnecting his scattered visual memories. The lady agrees: "You're right, it wasn't like that before. We had a lot of work done when we moved in. That was quite a while ago!"

Next we go out the back of the house. The little footbridge that Jacques often mentioned, which allowed access to the hill behind the building, is gone! "You see, my buddy Robert and I climbed here, up to the top. We spent whole afternoons playing on this slope. It was amazing!" He shares these memories with some excitement. Michel translates as we go along, and the children laugh listening to this tale from someone who played here long before them! Before leaving, we're kindly invited to drink coffee in the living room, where other reminders from the past teach us a bit more about the daily life of René, Zette, and their son, while they and other French military families peacefully "occupied" this quiet little spa town on the banks of the Lahn River in the early 1950s!

We follow the steps of our journey and stop in another city where Jacques and his parents lived. We're in Fritzlar now, in a radically different setting. The family lived in a group of large buildings we won't enter. Fritzlar is a very lovely city, but I won't spend time here talking about the timber-framed buildings. Tardi already has, several times throughout this book! During our visit to the archives, we'll be surprised while looking through the photos that Mr. Lohmann, the archivist, has made available to us: get-togethers, family celebrations, a Christmas tree, military parades, a brass band — in short, life in the French community, with its events, birthdays, and commemorations! Most of these photos are small. Jacques scrutinizes them, impatient to find some trace... his father's or his mother's face, perhaps, or a place or a person that he might be able to recognize...

Abruptly, I stop, stunned, because I have just recognized HIM! This gentle-faced child, almost solemn, even... this little boy with his haircut clean around his ears and his clearly hand-knitted sweater. "Look, it's you! It's you, I'm sure of it! Look!" I'm overwhelmed by the discovery of his face, this unexpected gift emerging from a small stack of unidentified photos! Everyone clusters around us, each taking their turn to lean over the small photo and add a comment: "Oh, sure, that could be you!" Or: "Really? It does look like him, but how can you be sure?" And Jacques, a bit skeptical: "You really think that's me? I don't recognize myself!" But I identify him with certainty: the little boy with the gentle, thoughtful face, turning in circles with his teacher and friends... No hesitation: it's him. In the end, he'll agree that it is!

Unfortunately, we don't have the original photo, which remains in the city archives, and the quality of the copy is far from perfect. Too bad, but we'll have to be content with it, because it's the only one we found. What matters is that Tardi was able to find traces of his early childhood in Germany: the familiar setting of a spa town, a corridor and a hill where he had fun playing, the rooms where he saw himself again with his parents, René and Zette, still young — and the face of the boy he used to be!

—Dominique Grange (October 2018)

TOP
Tardi the cowboy.

BOTTOM
The face of the boy
he used to be!

Thank you to Mrs. Susanne Brandt; Mr. Jürgen Preuss; Mr. Hans Feih; Mr. Clemens Lohmann and his spouse, Mrs. Bermal Ikiyek; Mr. Wilfried Dieterichs (our first contact, who found the house in Bad Ems and sent photos in December 2013). Thanks to the Nell Family in Sigmaringen for photos of the city. Thank you to Hildegard and Michel Gosselin, always ready to freeze their feet off, translate, call, and contact the right people. They were dear to me. —Tardi

TOP
Right to left: Jürgen Preuss, Dominique Grange, Tardi, Michel and Hildegard Gosselin, Hans Feih.
© Anke Laumann / HNA

BOTTOM
In Bad Wildungen.

STALAG IIB GLOSSARY

P. 22

Inspired by the Model T, a car so common on the road it was known as the "Road Louse," French engineer Henri Mignet designed a small, easy to manufacture plane — dubbed the "Louse of the Sky" or the "Flying Flea." Having tested various prototypes of the aircraft during the '20s, Mignet had his first successful flight in 1933. However, his plans to mass-produce the Flying Flea never panned out. His 1934 book *Le Sport de l'Air* contained such complete instructions on how to construct this simple plane that hundreds of aviation enthusiasts around the world built it themselves at home.

P. 81

The First French Army arrived in southern France in the summer of 1944, following the Allied invasion of Provence (Operation Dragoon). In conjunction with the Sixth U.S. Army Group, they marched north, liberating various French cities along the way. During its combat operations, the First Army crossed the Rhine and Danube, and was therefore referred to by the names of these mighty rivers. Here, René mocks the pretention inherent in such a nickname.

P. 89

After the French Army was defeated by German forces, de Gaulle and the Free French turned to France's overseas colonies for assistance to end the German occupation. Thus, regiments were assembled made up of Spahis, troops recruited from the indigenous populations of Algeria, Tunisia, and Morocco. After campaigning in Italy, France, and Germany, the 3rd Algerian Regiment of Reconnaissance Spahis ultimately aided the First French Army in liberating Paris.

P. 104

Hailing from Loveresse, Switzerland, Grock, the alias of Charles Adrien Wettach (1880–1959), was one of the most popular and highly paid clowns in early 20th-century Europe. A talented musician, his signature act involved blunders with a piano and violin. He bid farewell to the stage with a final performance in Hamburg, Germany, on October 30, 1954.

P. 115

In the second half of the second word balloon on this page, Jacques is referring to, respectively, Chevalier de Bayard, a chivalrous French figure of the late 15th and early 16th centuries dubbed "The Good Knight"; one of the three heroic swordsmen in Alexandre

STALAG IIB GLOSSARY

Dumas' classic 1844 novel *The Three Musketeers*; the protagonist of Victor Hugo's epic 1862 novel *Les Misérables*; the Roman slave and gladiator famous for leading a slave revolt; Fanfan la Tulip, a charismatic rogue and title character of the eponymous 1952 comedy adventure film set in 18th-century France; Robert Surcouf, a brazen French privateer who terrorized the Indian Ocean in the late 18th and early 19th centuries; Louis Mandrin, a famed highwayman known as the "Robin Hood" of France.

P. 134

Created by Louis Forton, the comic book series *The Slackers* (*Les Pieds Nickelés*) debuted in the newspaper *L'Épatant* on June 4, 1908. The series starred three lazy yet goodhearted brothers whose scheming ways led to all kinds of anarchic misadventures. Here, Jacques refers to the artist René Pellos, who took over the series in 1948 (with scriptwriter Roland de Montaubert).

French cartoonist Edmond-François Calvo was known for his various comic book series aimed at young readers. Here, Jacques is likely referring to Calvo's magnum opus, *The Beast Is Dead!* (1944), a two-volume graphic novel depicting WWII through the lens of woodland creatures.

P. 135

In 1942, the artist Raymond Peynet took a trip to Valence, where he sat on a park bench facing an ornate bandstand. Letting his mind wander, he dreamed up the vision of a violinist playing in the bandstand to an audience of one — a lovely young woman listening intently. His first illustrations featuring these characters appeared in the humor magazine *Ric et Rac* in 1944, and ever since imagery of this iconic couple have been ubiquitous throughout France, appearing on everything from postage stamps to porcelain. The famous bandstand in Valence was classified as a historical monument in 1982 to celebrate the artist and his famous "lovers."

TRANSLATOR: Jenna Allen | EDITOR: Conrad Groth | DESIGNER: Jacob Covey | SUPERVISING EDITOR: Gary Groth
PRODUCTION: Christina Hwang | ASSOCIATE PUBLISHER: Eric Reynolds | PUBLISHER: Gary Groth

Fantagraphics Books, Inc. | 7563 Lake City Way NE | Seattle, WA 98115

www.fantagraphics.com | Facebook.com/Fantagraphics | @fantagraphics.com

ISBN: 978-1-68396-366-0 | Library of Congress Control Number: 2017957109 | First Fantagraphics Books edition: November 2020

PRINTED IN CHINA